Con
Humanities

Spring 2018

Question More
www.cchumanities.org

The Community College Humanities Association (CCHA), founded in 1979, is the only national organization of its kind for humanities faculty and administrators in two-year colleges. It is dedicated to preserving and strengthening the humanities in two-year colleges.

CCHA serves as a catalyst for defining the issues which face humanities faculty and administrators today, finding solutions to problems in the field, and establishing a communications network for humanists. The Community College Humanities Review is a publication of CCHA. Submission guidelines can be found at our website: www.cchumanities.org

Cover design / consultation: Dan Koperski
Interior design / consultation: Garrett Brooks

Copyright © 2018 CCHA
All rights reserved. Permission required.
Printed with CreateSpace.
ISBN: 978-1718652927
www.cchumanities.org

CCHA c/o Community College of Baltimore County
7201 Rossville Blvd., Baltimore, MD, 21237

Community College
Humanities Review

Spring 2018

Spring 2018

" Hard times are coming, when we'll be wanting the voices of writers who can see alternatives to how we live now, can see through our fear-stricken society and its obsessive technologies to other ways of being, and even imagine real grounds for hope. We'll need writers who can remember freedom – poets, visionaries – realists of a larger reality.

—**Ursula K. Le Guin**, 2014 National Book Awards receiving the Medal for Distinguished Contribution to American Letters

The West Edge

by Sydney J. Elliott

Every Friday, my friend Joy and I would walk our dogs in Forest Park, located within the city limits of Portland, Oregon. On the way to our favorite trail-head, we passed a large but understated estate I was told was writer Ursula K. LeGuin's home. To be totally honest, I never saw her there, but I found my eyes resting on the front porch a moment longer than the other houses, and something would surge inside, knowing that she could be in there, working on another essay or novel.

I did have the opportunity to work with her and interview her for my university's newspaper while I was doing my undergrad at Portland State University. Our dance program was choreographing a performance based on her book, *Always Coming Home*, and she was at rehearsal as a consultant. I wrote reviews for the paper and nearly minored in dance (and for those who have seen me on the club floor, this may seem like an impossibility). But as someone who was majoring in English, as a fledgling woman writer, I was already an Ursula fan. We spent several rehearsals together talking about her book, dance, and art. This was over 20 years ago. I would run into her from time to time at various literary functions in Portland. Always kind. Always interested, a hand usually up to her face, taking in the situation, but never projecting fame. She was a voice for writers everywhere, for women in particular, and her work will endure.

I heard her daughter talk about her writing space in that big house. A tiny room under the stairs. The daughter was quick to note there were windows along one side, but the room itself was tiny. The small space could not, however, contain her unending creativity. Even Ursula herself, when asked, lost track of the number of books she had published.

I think of her there; I remember the surge I felt just knowing she and her words were near, and I want to capture that energy and keep it when times seem dark, when the news and media does its best to stifle my creativity, my voice. And it's been a powerful urge to cease as overwhelming reports of violence on people and art and civility pour forth, and my keyboard stays silent, too tired as yet another school shooting happened this morning. My heart sometimes says, harbor your energy, you can't compete with all this, go to work, teach, grade, and keep your head down.

I am weary. I know many of us are. When I heard that Ursula had passed away, I located *Dancing on the Edge of the World*, a collection of talks and essays. It was given to me by a bicyclist from Colorado. He was riding the coastal route near where I now live by himself after being dumped in Seattle by his girlfriend. I met him in line at the store. He had been drinking and told the checker he was planning to ride to a nearby town. It was nearly dark, and too many bicyclists are killed on our narrow winding roads, so I took him home. He talked. I listened. He slept on the creaky futon with my cat.

The next morning, I went to work, and I don't know where he kept it (he had only a backpack), but he left the book with a note in the cover, thanking me for being kind. For listening.

So, I garner my courage. Even a small space can create a masterpiece. The smallest act can inspire. We need to keep picking up the pen, hitting the keys, leading and teaching our students, making art, and harness the power we all have to bring light to those who need it.

(And yes, I still dance.)

Cheers,

Sydney J. Elliott
Editor
sydneyelliott@tillamookbaycc.edu

Unbeaten Paths

by Andrew Rusnak Jr.

The humanities are more about questions than answers.

The objective for studying any core discipline in the humanities is to provide a comprehensive and balanced education in order to:

- Educate the whole person to build a life, not just the skilled employee to build a career;
- Cultivate free and independent thinking;
- Nurture critical thinking, complex and creative problem solving, and analytic reasoning;
- Encourage empathetic response;
- Comprehend the difference between good and bad judgement while simultaneously calculating risk;
- Understand diversity and cultures outside the U.S.;
- Develop strong and effective communication skills;
- Inspire civic responsibility; and
- Most important, search for the next significant question.

There are a slew of other reasons, and you can see I've borrowed some common phrases that notables have uttered when the debate of humanities vs. other disciplines and specific job training comes up, which it has throughout modern history. Roughly, starting with the Huxley/Arnold debates in the late 1800s, the dispute proceeded through the publication C.P. Snow's *The Two Cultures* published in 1959, and can be said to be culminating in today's cultural and political arguments concerning what an education should be and what should be funded and what should not. The proposed defunding of the National Endowment for the Humanities is an indication of the hostile climate.

Every now and then, those of us who hold close to the flame of humanities need to remind ourselves of why what we advocate, what most of us celebrate way beyond a simple career choice, is important. Sometimes, however, in so doing, we lock ourselves into that same, automatic, routine, response. It's left to wonder whether today what we are defending, while still important in an increasingly undefined sense, might need more than its normal reawakening. The current debate and subsequent defense of the humanities does not seem at all like it is part of the same historical cycle of conflict that has gone before. There are new and more profound variables to be considered that are undermining the very cognitive skills listed above that the humanities depend on. Do we not need them any longer? Is our culture changing so rapidly that what we refer to as the traditional humanities disciplines and the cognitive skills they instill are no longer required? Is there no such thing as a "whole" person or "free" and "independent" thinking? The go-to, neuro-based progenitors of contemporary thought would argue that the "self" as we have indeed known it, is an illusion.

At no other time in history has the question "What does it mean to be human?" been so important and in need of a stable answer. Technology has changed the human condition before, but today, with accelerated advances in artificial intelligence, biotechnology and genetic engineering, nano-technology, and communications, humanity is being pushed into a vortex that leaves little for the time-honored, time-consuming, humanities education-inspired tradition of reflection and contemplation. It is, more than ever, still imperative for us in the humanities to ask the question, "What does it mean to be human, or, to become more human?" But it may not be right for us any longer to respond, simply, by saying that we should read more Shakespeare, study more Kant, or read more David McCullough. Is it not true that, even if we cannot respond definitively that at least we sense the answers to the "What does it mean to be human?" question were different a century ago? And, will be different a half-century from now? What place the humanities? What are the humanities today?

Question: Are the humanities adequately responding to the question, "What does it mean to be human today?

Sincerely,

Andrew Rusnak Jr., Executive Director, Publisher
Arusnak@ccbcmd.edu

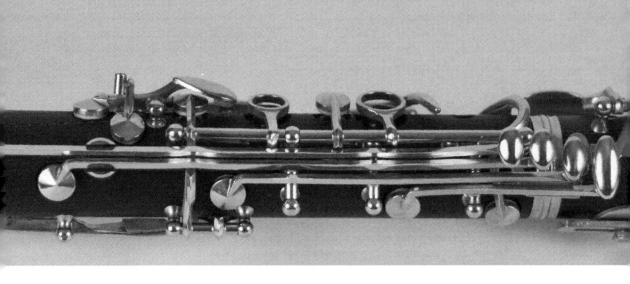

On Brutal Auditions, the Exigencies of Spring, and the Life of Professor Christopher Wolfe

by Andrew Rusnak Jr.

The audition is the tomb or the treetop. Fail it and it can define your life. Pass it and it can define your life. Opportunity and death knell, it gathers everything you know about yourself and ties it into an ever-tighter knot until it is as dense as the universe at the beginning of time with no room for redemption. Myriad elements with no purpose arrange themselves in myriad ways. Auditions are when the higher-level intent of organized precision clashes with self-destructive chaos in an attempt to reckon the question of, 'How did I get here?' with the questions: 'What is objective? What is subjective?' And, 'What is an illusion?' For one is trying to pass on to others the mirror one holds up to one's self before it breaks.

It was, perhaps, the biggest, most defining audition of his life, the few he'd already completed and the many yet to come, the approved, confident, practiced equation of success vs. the inevitable, unknown, ubiquitous demons of uncertainty.

By spring 1963, Chris Wolfe's immediate future was set. For the past five years, he'd attended the prestigious Peabody Conservatory studying clarinet and orchestral conducting. Founded as the Peabody Institute in 1857, absorbed by The Johns Hopkins University in 1985, the college is an internationally renowned literary and cultural center that graduated many notable classical musicians.

By fall of '63, Wolfe would be on his way to Vienna. He'd graduated first in his class and had survived the grueling application process to win a Fulbright Scholarship. In Austria, he would study under the internationally acclaimed clarinetist Willi Boskovsky.

Surprisingly, however, a rare clarinet position opened up with the then-fledgling Baltimore Symphony Orchestra (BSO). Wolfe's ultimate goal was to become a full-time clarinetist. He thought it best to take the audition, for experience, knowing that navigating these tests of nerve and skill were the only rite de passage into the world of the professional orchestral musician.

"I told my Fulbright sponsor, Dr. Elliot Galkin, who taught music history at Peabody that I was going to take the audition," said Wolfe. "He said I should."

Most of the BSO musicians taught at Peabody to supplement their income, but this did not advantage Wolfe in any way, even though he took lessons from Principal Clarinetist, Iggy Gennusa. There were close to 50 musicians from all over the country who took the same audition. In the first round, they were all given a number, placed behind a screen, and told to play a number of selections, including Mozart's clarinet concerto.

"You sit there and listen to all these great clarinetists and think you're nowhere near as good as they are," Wolfe says, shaking his head. "Auditions are brutal. Each one takes a year off your life."

Perhaps because there are so few clarinet jobs that ever open up. A cursory scan of a recent copy of *International Musician*, the monthly journal of the American Federation of Musicians of the United States and Canada, revealed only one rather obscure, available position.

Only six final candidates would survive the prelims and be asked to play an additional round. Somehow Wolfe's number was called. The screen came down and there sat Music Director, Peter Herman Adler along with all the principal players from every section of the BSO.

"I played and the others played," recalls Wolfe. "In the end they asked me if I wanted the job. I had to really think about it, I didn't want to burn any bridges with Fulbright because they are hard to get. After a few days, because it is what I ultimately wanted to do, I took the job."

In 2015, after 52 years, four of which were spent as assistant conductor, Wolfe retired from the BSO. In the early years, the Boston Pops hired the BSO to tour the American south, part of a scant 28-week schedule for the young ensemble. Musicians had to supplement their incomes any creative way they could. It wasn't until Romanian-born Music Director, Sergio Comissiona took over and Joseph and Harvey Meyerhoff built a concert hall in the early 1980s that, for the first time, the BSO enjoyed a 52-week season.

He thought it best to take the audition, for experience, knowing that navigating these tests of nerve and skill were the only rite de passage into the world of the professional orchestral musician.

Wolfe travelled all over the world to play. Along the way, however, he developed another passion, to teach and organize youth bands and orchestras as a music professor at the Community College of Baltimore County (CCBC).

"Would you like to sit for an interview, for a story on your life and career? Two careers really."

With a wry smile, Chris Wolfe cocks his head a little to the right, then down, apparently pleased with the question but clearly feigning insouciance.

"Sure, I can help out," he says, thoughts spinning.

The keen and tough-minded Wolfe, 76, always seems a couple steps ahead of normal conversation, let alone any amped up banter.

"It'll get pretty detailed, deep into who you are, your …"

"What do you want me to do, take my clothes off?"

The bon mot is vintage post-WWII culture, with roots in the industrial work ethic that built the first half of the 20th century.

"I was born on Christmas day, 1940," Wolfe said, then pads the tale, jesting, "My mother said I was the worst present she ever got." Vintage, follow-up amusement, not exactly studio laughter, but timely.

He is good at word darts, timely, spiked comebacks more tuned to an era when the P.C. and literati weren't peddling hypersensitive trigger warnings, micro-aggressions, and power-based critical theory. A raw sense of humor might have been considered a necessary survival skill back in the proverbial day to offset a dire and more emotionally-plagued daily life. Wolfe now has twin freshman college students, in their late teens, both on full rides at the University of Maryland.

"Yeah go ahead, take off your clothes, embarrass yourself, but step out into the hall first."

There's a triptych of Wolfe attached to a 1985 article in the Baltimore Symphony Orchestra's magazine, *Overture*. In the first panel he's fielding a question, an inquisitive, on-it expression. In the second he's responding with much animation, hand up, fingers spread as if he's ready to bang some piano keys. In the third, with a mischievous sure grin, he's gauging the reaction of the interviewer, the ready prankster part of his personality within easy reach in case the interview needs to be saved from becoming too sober, deliberate, or even penetrating.

The ludic Wolfe hasn't changed much. He especially scurries to be out front. He always seems to be running. What he's running to has been more obvious in his life and career than what he's running from. The course is mostly round with long linear stretches.

On a warm spring afternoon in 1954, towheaded freshman Christopher Wolfe quickly pressed through the not-too-crowded halls of Herndon High School in Virginia a little late for track practice. It'd been several years since Harry Wolfe, in an attempt to recapture the pastoral impressions of his West Virginia roots, moved his family from Germany to Great Falls. Initially, Christopher struggled to acclimate, but now enjoyed a network of friends and status as an honors student. Excited about his next race, he could almost smell the fresh-cut grass and hay from the nearby farms that surrounded the school.

"I ran the 800," he says. "I think it's the most grueling race, in between the long sprint of the 400 and the long-distance pace of the 1,500. I also ran the 440 relay and the cross-country mile. Didn't have the marathon back then, we didn't dare run in the street. Cars would run you down."

As he squirted past the music room, a cacophony of sounds caught his ear. There was nothing particularly tagged music in his past outside several years of unwanted and tedious piano lessons in Germany where his father was stationed right after WWII, and his mother's singing and accordion playing. Mary Wolfe played impromptu gatherings in bombed-out bunkers as a USO volunteer to raise canned goods (German marks were meaningless) for German youth who were woefully underfed, some were starving, orphaned children who spent days foraging for basic subsistence through tons of rubble that overwhelmed the Nuremberg landscape.

Compelled to poke his head through the door, Wolfe was met with a question that would set the direction of his life for the next 60-plus years.

"Do you play an instrument?" Mr. Lester, the faculty band director asked Wolfe.

"No, I played a little piano when I was younger," Wolfe replied, probably recollecting how that didn't go too well after he slammed the wooden keyboard cover on his instructor's fingers.

"Well, I need someone to play the clarinet, are you interested?"

That day, Wolfe dragged an old metal clarinet to track practice, a giveaway from a military band in Washington, DC. Hundreds of thousands of metal clarinets had been manufactured in the first half of the 20th century, many of which were eventually donated to music programs in schools.

"I took it home and started practicing, or more like squeaked and squawked on it," said Wolfe "My father, who was tone deaf, wasn't very happy.

Christopher Wolfe.

For Wolfe, the idea of practice became a life-long obsession, right up until his retirement.

"Three hours a day, everyday," he said. "That's what one of my teachers told me. Twenty-one hours a week. I was practicing much more than that as a student at Peabody. You can't have the horn out of your mouth or your muscles will atrophy."

Wolfe started the night he took home Lester's clarinet. *Sing, Sing, Sing* and *Jersey Bounce* and *Air Mail Special,* the final vestiges of the golden era of radio and swing king bebopper Benny Goodman, who popularized the clarinet, had by now been moved to the classical charts only to be resurrected by Wolfe whose newly bred, fledgling appreciation for jazz ensembles grew exponentially. He'd later catch up to *I Got Rhythm* and the Goodman Quartet on the newer medium of television. Lester, also a "jazzer," continued to hear whatever arcane confluence of variables aligned to inspire Wolfe's budding flair for jazz and classical music, and came to the conclusion when Wolfe was still only in the 9th grade that his young talent would soon evolve beyond his ability to teach him. The ambitious Wolfe would need private lessons. Only an honest mentor completely in touch with his or her knowledge bank and skills as a teacher could put aside ego to pass on taking any credit for what may turn out to be one of the better recent discoveries in high school music.

To spend close to half of your conscious life sitting in a hard chair drawing on the primeval promise of music through a deceptively beguiling and tapered mouthpiece, fighting the tyranny of irregular breathing, staring at sheet music on a metal stand, deserves at least some access to a higher-level honesty. Wolfe readily admits, in the highly competitive world of symphony music, when someone may have been a better musician. But, during the countless hours of mundane practice, whatever limitations of talent and endurance went through the gauntlet of self-discovery, it still comes off as a cultivated delusion because it duels with another immanent awareness of Wolfe's, that there exists—in a binding existential covenant—that vague cache of raw untapped will, that no one really knows their limitations or what they are capable of accomplishing.

"You just can't do that anymore," says a much younger fellow-CCBC Music Professor, Dan Lewis, who plays guitar and keyboards. "You can't go directly from graduating conservatory to a professional symphony job."

Wolfe determined his own destiny, stuck to the formula. Today's American Dream, however, with its conventional decrees confronting a flood of fleeting, protean variables and ultimately disillusioned ideas, seems a much harder sell. The formula has indeed changed. There may be even more "success," whatever that has come to mean, but certainly less guarantees. Hard work seems to have been taken out of the equation and social media hits on minimal talent based on spectacle seems to have been inserted. It's like sleepwalking one's way, not to success, but simply, a species of satisfaction based on short attention spans. Wolfe says that real auditions are much more intense than American Idol. "You have to know a full repertoire of music." Reality TV, the commodification of happenstance and frivolity, cell phones and immediate reward have all vanquished self-awareness, individuation, and the infinite spirit of possibility. Does Wolfe have any passionate students who practice relentlessly, inspired to meet a single, self-defining goal?

The fearful refrain included his father's persuasive suggestion to study engineering in college. It may have been background music at the time, but when it came to making a decision, the pragmatic and the patriotic won out over the fortuitous life of a musician.

Improvised backbeats and fills break the end-of-semester silence from a studio room across the hall where a student is practicing the drums. After a long roll, Wolf takes pause. He knows the student.

"That kid has lot of potential," he says listening. "He's really good. I gave him copies of jobs he could apply for, to get started, marching band stuff. Trouble is, he wants to be a rock star."

Wolfe's may be the last generation to fully project and imagine the influence of regret as a motivating, practice till you bleed, linear path to success. Now the more realized version of his colleagues' concurrence of "sincere, unpretentious, and dedicated," cited in the '85 *Overture* piece, Wolfe still connects dots the old fashioned way, being very forthright about Lester's early influence on his nascent ambition as a clarinetist and later as a music professor at the Community College of Baltimore County.

"He was the perfect example of how a teacher's influence can have a long-term effect on a student," said Wolfe. "Without him I would not have taken this path."

Lester, who'd played trombone in Les Brown's jazz band, called clarinetist Sidney

Forrest to arrange an audition for Wolfe to start lessons. Forrest, a recognized virtuoso, played principal clarinet with the National Symphony Orchestra and taught at Catholic University and the Peabody Conservatory.

"He had a studio in Washington, DC, in DuPont Circle," Wolfe remembers. "This is what started the whole thing for me. He was a wonderful teacher. He made me practice and I was scared to death if I wasn't prepared for my lessons. I started playing in the high school band in 10th grade."

Despite, however, Wolfe's passion for the indulgent sounds of the clarinet, his lust for jazz, and zealous proclivity for practice—a well-tuned, gritty response to obstacles is to practice even more—add high school girlfriends, Benny Goodman on the radio, and summer jobs bailing hay, picking greenhouse tomatoes, and digging foundations for his father's construction business, popular American culture in the mid-to-late 1950s, somewhat like today, started to respond to new norms, away from the arts and humanities toward engineering and technology.

Like today, the proposition is either the clarinet or the microscope, humanities and arts, or STEM. Lost is the idea that the cognitive skills a variety of disciplines inspire feed off and need each other for any one of them to be fully developed and successful (arts and humanities would make a comeback in the turbulent late 60s). But, WWII was only 10 years in the rearview mirror, and the Cold War with the Soviet Union was finding an alarming new gear. The "never-seen-before," Soviet-launched satellite Sputnik, exacerbated Americans' already deep underlying fear of "the bomb" and advanced a desperation that spread like a virus carried by the ubiquity and powerful new influence of television. Eisenhower confirmed the threat.

David Hoffman, director of the documentary *Sputnik Mania*, was quoted by CBS in 2007: "I can't think of a time when we were that afraid, even at Pearl Harbor, even at 9/11."

Hoffman went on to say: "When I was in college, I read a Life Magazine account…. They went to some high school in Chicago, I believe, and showed my generation out there—dancing and all the frivolity. And then the Soviet student is shown working at his desk on calculus at midnight, with a light bulb over his head. Our entire educational structure changed. All over America, boys by the thousands wanted to help America win, beat the Russians."

Sputnik provoked Americans. They looked up and over their shoulders. The cure for angst became not "the only thing we have to fear is fear itself," but a tangible fix, one unclouded by abstraction. Engineering and technology can provide clarity, albeit sometimes too much. Young men put away the trumpets and clarinets. Instead they built and launched thousands of model rockets and the space race was on.

Wolfe, for a long while, heard this song playing in the ear of America's future. The fearful refrain included his father's persuasive suggestion to study engineering in college. It may have been background music at the time, but when it came to making a decision, the pragmatic and the patriotic won out over the fortuitous life of a musician. Swing time was avocation. So, in his senior year at Herndon High, he applied to the University of Virginia and was accepted. He would pursue a degree in mechanical engineering.

In the '85 *Overture* profile, Wolfe is described as having a "down-to-earth, low-key manner, [that] belies the image of the performer as prima donna" (it was the 80s after all). These days, Chris Wolfe can't sit still. He roams the halls of the Arts and Humanities building on the campus of CCBC on his way to teach a music appreciation class, or pay one of his liberal arts colleagues a visit. Even if only delivering a message for something as trivial as a meeting time, he'd rather do it in person than use email. The writer in the '85 piece, when

Wolfe was 43, claimed he was "determined to keep his feet on the ground."

Idioms aside, 34 years later, Wolfe will jump up from his well-organized desk (he claims it's not)—plaques, photos, accolades illuminating his storied career as a musician, professor, conductor, and general all-around 'helper outer' decorating the wall—and make his way to someone's office for a chat. Often the talk turns to the Baltimore Orioles and Ravens (he's a season ticket holder), Trump's position on climate change, the virtues of a community college education, something he heard on the radio, the perils of racism, or his kids' volunteer work in foreign countries.

"Chris will stop by my office to give me grief about the Pittsburgh Steelers, segue into giving me serious career and institutional advice (and it's worth listening to), then he'll say, 'Alright, well, your Steelers still suck' and go about his day," says fellow Humanities Professor, Greg Campbell, laughing. "He's one of a kind and I don't know what we'd do without him."

Students humor over the noisy contrast between his loud, music-motifed shirts and ties. Amiable, keen, sometimes prickly and irascible, he's a welcome sight, an opportunity for face-to-face conversation, relief from a world that would rather put its head down and thumb its way through a text, a world that now packages the thorny responsibility of human relationships in binary code.

When he vigorously goes on his way, he'll leave a hearty laugh that resonates until the next time he stops by.

In 1946, immediately following the end of WWII, Harry Wolfe, a business school graduate from the University of West Virginia now an attaché for the U.S. State Department, moved from Aberdeen Proving Ground in Maryland, where his in-laws happened to reside and where he was stationed as a member of the militia (somewhat equivalent to today's National Guard), to Nuremburg, Germany.

Due to bad eyesight, during the war years Harry could not serve in the regular Army, but now had the opportunity to take part in a puissant historical event, a series of military tribunals that held 22 prominent Nazi war criminals accountable for wanton acts of inhumanity—the Nuremburg trials. A year later, after Chris completed first grade, Mary moved the rest of the family to Germany where they remained until 1952, two-and-a-half years in Nuremberg, two-and-a-half in Stuttgart.

"He was very secretive about it all," Chris remembers. "My father couldn't and didn't say much about the trials, so we learned not to ask and just lived with the secrecy. We never found out exactly what he did. To be honest I think he actually hated it."

Wolfe eventually tells a story of how much he despised German youth when he lived in Nuremberg and Stuttgart, how one of the neighborhood bullies, feeding off the pervading bitterness that ran rampant in the post-war ethos, threw a rock at him and busted his head, a scar he still has, and how, thereafter, he had to travel in packs of American kids to get to school. Several days later, not wanting to create the wrong impression, he makes it a point to follow up on the story. He wants to be sure it's clear that he had a great childhood, "nothing at all to complain about."

Wolfe's look back starts to shake out to something like Uncle Sam's finger pointing propaganda of depravation and sacrifice. Honor, humility, and patriotism connect to the Platonic abstraction of virility, a black or white, right or wrong Weltanschauung that laments the retreat of the breadwinner father, regrets the passing of sinewy forearms tattooed with the names of WWII Navy ships, indelible blue and red ink smeared by time and a hard sun, muscles stretched and undulating as they reached for wrenches and screwdrivers on Saturday mornings before disappearing under the hoods of old Chevys in a neighbor's backyard.

But Wolfe reached for a clarinet in a black tux much of the time. What it means to be a man in the zeitgeist of the American 50s started to become a different question than what did my father expect of me. The Robert Wilson archetype the mid-20th century American male inherited, the professional hunter and guide and lothario in Hemingway's "The Short and Happy Life of Francis Macomber," was already beginning to fade to obsolescence and cliché in a world that embraced "going to the office," and a culture that would come to celebrate, as

What it means to be a man in the zeitgeist of the American 50s started to become a different question than what did my father expect of me.

a variety of brands of normal, the absurd, the spectacle, the ephemeral, ubiquitous media and commodification, and gender neutrality.

"My mother had a master's in math from College Park," he said. "She was the head stenographer for the World Bank in Washington, DC. Don't put this in the article, but she made more money than my father, it always upset him."

Then Wolfe's kinetic, locker-room laugh, razzes his long-dead father in a respectable way, but not without dropping the inextricable angst of place and self. "My father never came to my opening when I started with the BSO," Wolfe said.

Wolfe came to be in one world, a world of pin ups in tool boxes, not clarinet cases. And he watches over his kids in another. He has no hesitation sending them on deep immersion expeditions to live for weeks at a time with penurious village families in Latin America and Africa to fulfill more-than-required community service requirements for college and career goals. It's a way of putting them in touch with the steep economic and social boundaries that surrounded him as a child in Europe and the U.S. after the depression, after the war. "I've got to learn Spanish," he'll proclaim, to keep up with his kids. And, with a furrowed brow and a look of deep revulsion after the recent white supremacist protests in Charlottesville, "There's no room for prejudice, I saw what happened in Germany."

What lingers? What vestiges? The lucky-to-be-more-fortunate adaptation of a Grapes of Wrath descendant?

What lingers? What vestiges? The lucky-to-be-more-fortunate adaptation of a Grapes of Wrath descendant? The inequitable fruits of relentless productivity joined to the Great Depression pain of repetition, suppression, reticence? It all fits, during random conversation, when Wolfe suddenly proclaims how "spoiled" America is today, a theme he grinds from a proletariat angle before issuing that signature seasoned laugh of reassurance. He knows because spoiled is something he was once guilty of. He knows because of where he's been—there were 53 air raids over Stuttgart, the heat so intense it ignited a conflagration that left 1.5 million cubic meters of rubble. He knows that haunting place in history that suddenly reduced human relationships to Auschwitz and Hiroshima, a time when the promise of human empathy gave way to the twisted "rationality" of systematic mass murder. He's witness to more than half the 20th century and almost a quarter of the 21st—prop planes to Watson. He likes what he likes, disses what he doesn't. When it comes to the new sport of media-inspired political campaigns, many Baby Boomers, Xers, and Millennials see exploitation and an almost comical illusion relegated to resurrections of atavistic tribal sensibilities.

With more seasoned sentiment, those of the GI generation are apt to be seduced, although not indoctrinated, by that flicker of fiber that built the industrial world and rebuilt Europe through the Marshall Plan after the war, not submissive because they've seen it all before, they know where the line is. Wolfe is proud of his letters of recommendation from that generation of Maryland politicos—Hutchinson, Tydings, Mathias, Muth.

"There was a lot of destruction in Germany when the war ended, and a lot of military," said Wolfe. "The house we lived next to in Stuttgart was flattened, nothing but rubble. Streetcars were running, but every other house was destroyed—a lot of destruction and a lot of poverty. We didn't feel too sorry for the German people because of what they did. They didn't like us either. I had one friend, Peter who lived next door. He taught me some German and we kicked around the soccer ball every now and then."

Wolfe's mother started a cub scout pack for the American children. She held parties for many of her husband's associates. Every weekend, the family travelled around Europe—France, Austria, Italy.

"I didn't learn much, 2nd, 3rd, 4th, 5th grade," Wolfe laments the American schools on military bases. "I missed whatever instruction I would've received in the states, especially in subjects like world geography. What I learned was from the streets, from travelling. I saw a lot of things. Those memories still come back."

Despite the charred ruins and enmity for Americans, young Chris enjoyed a somewhat charmed life in Germany as many Germans were desperate for jobs. The Wolfe family employed a nanny, maids, and were well-attended, part of a privileged group of historically-cast people responsible for restoring a sense of coherence and altruism to a humanity broken by a seductive, nationalist-driven cult of megalomania. Reinforced by

the family narrative he carries around in his memory bank, Wolfe now uses the term on himself, a common enough contemporary trap he wants his kids to avoid—"spoiled."

"I had some difficult times when we moved to Great Falls Virginia," Wolfe says. "I'd been all over the world and now we were surrounded by farmland. Lots of the kids thought I was conceited. After Germany, we were supposed to go to Liberia, but my father had enough seniority to transfer out of the State Department and into the Defense Department. He was stationed at Fort Mead as a manpower analyst. My father grew up in West Virginia. He loved to hunt and fish. He didn't want to live in Maryland. It was a tough commute back then, to Fort Meade. I think that's what contributed to his untimely death, he had heart problems."

Harry Wolfe retired from government service in 1956 at the age of 55 to build houses and start a real estate business. He died of heart disease at 62.

"Granddaddy Wolfe also died very young, he had a premature heart attack in his 40s," Wolfe says. "My father had two brothers who died of heart disease in their late 50s. All the Wolfes died. My father walked through the door of one of the houses he was building had a massive stroke. Thank God my mother's side had better genes. They all lived into their 80s."

One way or the other, if you want to find reasons why you shouldn't keep on, you'll find 'em. The obstacles are all there; there are a million of 'em.

— Benny Goodman

Frankfurt School critical theorist Theodor Adorno, in his essay *On the Fetish Character in Music and the Regression of Listening*, observed the nuanced distinctions made in the enhanced awareness of modern music's effects, writing "…[M]usic represents at once the immediate manifestation of impulse and the locus of its

Christopher Wolfe.

taming. It stirs up the dance of the Maenads and sounds from Pan's bewitching flute, but it also rings out from the Orphic lyre, round which the visions of violence range themselves, pacified."

Musicians need clarity, distinction, precision in temporal relationships. And, before the serendipitous arrangement of independent sounds abandons the presence of space to transcend all rational explanations of love, they also need to count, to find beat, a foundation. Running, three miles daily, there's a rhythm to Wolfe's thinking, a morphology, a mathematical arrangement, like sheet music—the feel of counting steps on concrete, grass, asphalt. Arch, heel, toe, like tapping to keep time. Chaos eventually finds a pulse. Reprise, and the win. Subdued "visions of violence" especially after the svelte Wolfe crossed the finish line of five marathons. He still out-scoots most humanities professors half-his age.

"There's nothing interesting about my life," he says repeatedly. Repeatedly. It's safe to assume the clarinet and the well-stitched, complex structure of classical music won out over the impulsive pluck of jazz (save the splashy, offbeat shirts), and mediated much of Wolfe's disposition. But as much as he's tempted to wrap his life up in the steady safe cadence of a metronome, sudden deflections give it away. First, laughing, soaking it up before flicking compliments into a nearby hole—a joke, a lull, a quick change of subject, even transgressive, politically incorrect quips. Impulsive Jazz makes a comeback. Spontaneity is essential to creativity, to wit. Football offers more extemporaneous opportunity to act than baseball and "I love football," he proclaims.

But, to most in his generation, egotism and vanity are odious and best served up in self-deprecating humor. It's a short synaptic jump from humility and resignation to empathy, unified goals, and chasing the kinds of dreams that were packaged in blue collar sensibilities in the 1950s.

"Sometimes it was hard to take a seat back in the orchestra, after conducting," he says, reflecting on the two roles of orchestrating and playing music. "I don't know about Apple, or Xerox or IBM, but a symphony orchestra is an autocratic environment, the music director rules everything. I had to be careful what I did on the podium. When you go back and sit down in your chair as a player after telling somebody what to do, that's tough. I was friendly with all of my colleagues, but there was jealousy and some whispers like, 'He shouldn't be conducting,' because they all wanted to conduct. But, they voted for me too. Most assistant conductors stay for four years and that's it. I ended up loving every minute of it."

So much so that in spring of 1989, Wolfe applied for a rare opening as Principal Conductor and Music Director for the Evansville, Indiana Philharmonic Orchestra. He had prepared hard for this moment of opportunity. He wanted to conduct full time. Seven years previous, he'd took second in the National Conducting Competition in La Crosse, Wisconsin, and in 1987, as the BSO's Assistant Conductor, he'd conducted, "An Evening with Mel Torme."

"I was ready to pick up and move my family," he said. "Moving is part of this business. It was a great job and I thought I had it in the bag."

"In between the Armenian bombshell . . . Loris Tjeknavorian, who electrified the crowd . . . and Wolfe, who drew a sustained standing ovation, there were three pretenders," wrote Evansville Sunday Courier Concert Reviewer Dave Rutter. "We have a genuine horse race . . .

for the 'Pick-Me-To-Replace-Stewart-Kershaw derby."

In the end, however, the job went to one of the pretenders. The emotional investment in the emotionally driven endeavor that is music can be undercut by the intermittent, superficial reality of messy political nepotism.

"Politics plays a role in getting jobs, boy does it ever," said Wolfe.

This was one audition that Wolfe would have to sacrifice to the "dance of the Maenads."

You can build all the monuments to culture and have well-paid maestros, but it's the people who play those musical contraptions called instruments, that's what makes the music.

—Chris Wolfe, to a standing-room only audience after conducting an improvised Baltimore Symphony Orchestra concert after the musicians were locked out by management for refusing to accept the terms of a new contract. Quote taken from the *Baltimore Sun.*

Again it is spring, the "cruelest" and most fortuitous season, when the Gods of Music intervene in Wolfe's life. It is 1958. Despite his commitment to the University of Virginia and the firm, quantifiable guarantees of mechanical engineering, Forrest arranged an audition for Wolfe at the Peabody Conservatory in Baltimore and talked him into going.

"My father hated the city," Wolfe remembers, laughing. "When we would visit my grandparents in Aberdeen, there were no beltways or I-95. We'd drive the parkway to Baltimore, took Franklin and turned right onto Orleans, which is Pulaski Highway. Every time we came down that hill, my father would start to rant and cuss about how dirty and ugly the city was, how he could never live here. He told me the last place I wanted to come was Baltimore, to take an audition."

The experience of auditions—the anxiety and insecurity, a half-hour test administered by strangers that could convert one's entire sense of self, status, and fate into loss, confusion, and spiritual desolation. Wolfe's first real test was auditioning for Forrest to take him on as a student. The second would be within the revered marble-columned halls of Peabody in historic Mount Vernon, the cultural hub of Baltimore. The nation's first monument to George Washington stood guard in the square across the street.

"There was no campus, only a monument," Wolfe says, still laughing. "There was a big Methodist church on one corner, and here's this big, ugly building with a museum on the other side. My mom drove me up and we were going to see my grandmom in Aberdeen afterwards, have a nice dinner. I was going to do this just to make Mr. Lester and Mr. Forrest happy."

When he reached the top of the stairs, he heard the familiar sounds of scales, aspiring students fingering their way through the upper and lower joints of the clarinet.

Like many adolescents, Wolfe, at times, warded off his solidifying sense of self determination. He questioned his love of playing the clarinet. In the back of his mind he knew UVA only had pep and marching bands, no real music program.

He made his way up a gothic spiral staircase avoiding the wrought-iron railings and "ugly" gray walls, something out of a "horror film," to the vaulted North Hall. Even in memory, as he relates the story, the fear is palpable and attenuates expectations. Wolfe had grown comfortable with his out, even convinced himself that his preference was to attend UVA and become an engineer, to be part of the celebrated race to space. But it's hard to listen to his story and not think he really wanted Peabody all along, despite the gloomy retrospect. After all he'd landed, physically and emotionally, in

the idyllic, verdant hills of Northern Virginia. Chris was sure he shared his father's distaste for the suffocating, uncompromising hard lines of city life.

When he reached the top of the stairs, he heard the familiar sounds of scales, aspiring students fingering their way through the upper and lower joints of the clarinet.

"You sit there and you wait and they call your name," Wolfe says. "We all had to play Mozart's clarinet concerto, in A major, the first movement, the biggest part of the audition. You walk into this big room, across the hall, the president's office. His name was Reginald Stewart. He was the music director for the Baltimore Symphony and the head of Peabody."

Flanked by the entire Peabody faculty fixed in straight-back chairs along the wall, Stewart, from England, attired in a well-tailored suit with a high collar shirt, cut an imposing figure. Like a steel beam, hands folded, he sat erect behind a finely-scrolled oak desk. In the middle of the windowless room, like a small island in the middle of a vast ocean, was a music stand and a chair. Wolfe took his position.

"What are you going to play for us young man?" said Stewart in an authoritative tone, despite that everyone played the same thing.

"I was a nervous wreck," says Wolfe. "My first thought was to get out of there."

Wolfe doesn't remember much about playing his bit. He does remember leaving, hurrying down the gothic staircase, the ugly gray walls a peripheral blur, his mother waiting outside with the car running, a welcome warm dinner waiting at grandmom's.

"Right before I reached the door handle of the car," Wolfe says, "some kid runs up and says, 'Hey Wolfe? Is your name Wolfe? They want to see you back in Stewart's office.' I went back and talked to him and all the rest of the faculty. Long story short . . . ."

It's a phrase—long story short—a diversion, when he becomes impatient with the rhythm of a conversation, or the detail slides into more positive light than he's comfortable with. Yet he was assistant conductor for the BSO for four years.

The faculty told Wolfe he played better than anyone else. They were going to offer him a full scholarship. In 1958 that meant $600 a year, compared to $46,000 today. Later that evening, when they returned home he told his father what had happened.

"He wasn't happy," Wolfe says, traces of lament now creeping into his voice. "My father didn't like music. I don't ever remember him humming a tune, whistling, or even singing the hymns in church where my mother was the choir director. He thought all musicians were 'fags.' Everything then was about Sputnik. It was almost treasonous to not be part of that. My father never came to my opening when I started with the Baltimore Symphony Orchestra, But I had a lot of support from my mother and grandmother."

Like many GI fathers, Harry Wolfe's notion of who and how he wanted his son to be was shaped by the Great Depression and WWII. Perhaps sensing the legacy of his own brutal work ethic, he would, however, hard though it may have been, acquiesce on Peabody if one condition was met. The free tuition not without standing, Christopher would also have to major in music education so he'd have some marketable skills after graduation.

That fall, Wolfe packed his bags, jumped the train to Baltimore, still worried about having made the right decision. Later, he'd laugh about not knowing anything about blacks, gays, Jews, the cultural diversity of urban life.

"I knew I had a friend there, my teacher and mentor Sidney Forrest, if anything went wrong, he would be there to take care of me," said Wolfe. "That was a good thing. If it had been anyone else? I don't know."

The kid that ran up to him the day of the audition turns out to be Les Lucko, who became a quick lifelong friend of Wolfe's and taught music for the Baltimore County School system.

Competing with his father's expectation to teach music was Chris' nascent desire to become a professional musician, to perform. To keep his end of the arrangement, he'd need to earn two degrees, one in applied music, the other in music education. Practice, practice, practice. No stranger to hard work, there was something he needed to prove, to get out in front of in hopes that later he could put it behind him. And it was only later, when he became a music professor, that he'd realize how important his father's advice had been.

Don't eat, don't sleep, don't date, don't bar hop, just practice, practice, practice. This was Wolfe's routine for five years.

The staid virago "Ma" Kennerly ran a boarding house for Peabody students, 707 St. Paul Street, catty-cornered to the college. Wolfe moved in.

"She fed us powdered eggs, and of course there was no alcohol or women allowed," Wolfe recalls. "At first, I had to block out the city of Baltimore. I went to my classes, I went to my practice room, I went to rehearsals, and I went to my dorm room and that was it. I went to summer music camps, in West Virginia, Michigan, and I auditioned and landed a spot for three summers with the American Wind Symphony in Pittsburgh, where we played on a barge where the three Rivers met. Music then became an obsession. There weren't many jobs out there, and what was out there didn't pay much."

After Peabody, Wolfe didn't always land summer gigs playing music, times when he

"was happy as a lark." (Yes, sometimes there's a slight Jimmy Stewart colloquialism.) When the first children arrived from his first marriage—he has five kids in all—he supplemented his income delivering newspapers, even (and he laughs hard at this one) sold women's lingerie door-to-door.

Ma Kennerly cut off practice for all students at 10pm sharp every night. Wolfe needed a part-time gig and up the street on Park Avenue, Emmanuel Episcopal Church needed a counter tenor for the all-male choir. He auditioned and got the job.

"The choir director gave me a key, that was the great thing about it," said Wolfe. "I could practice in the choir room until two or three in the morning."

Don't eat, don't sleep, don't date, don't bar hop, just practice, practice, practice. This was Wolfe's routine for five years. He had to take a lot of credits for both degrees, but despite missing a month of school his freshman year with pneumonia and mononucleosis, he graduated top of his class in 1963 winning the prestigious Horstmeyer Music Award.

He also gradually acclimated to city life, a much different, more amicable Baltimore than exists today, sometimes trekking all the way down to Howard Street after meeting his grandmother who'd take the B&O train from Aberdeen to the Mount Royal Station, now the site of the Maryland Institute College of Art, to meet Chris for lunch. The two then shopped the once popular downtown department stores—Hecht Co., Hoschild Kohn, Stewarts. When he recounts these nostalgic tales, "No one would bother you, you could go anywhere in the city, I loved those days with my grandmother," there are no restful interludes in Wolfe's voice, only elevated excitement sewn with traces of lament, not for his experience at Peabody, which would be the

best five years of his life, but for the lost soul of an American city, what today would be cynically interpreted as naïve suggestions to live in an equitable world devoid of prejudice and discrimination, a city he would come to represent for 52 years as a member of its namesake symphony.

He would, however, respond to the "immediate manifestation of impulse" and come to violate one measure of a somewhat sacred protocol that existed between students and mentors.

In the 1950s and early 60s, on twelve Wednesday nights throughout the year, at the Lyric Theater on Mount Royal Avenue not far from Peabody, the famed Philadelphia Orchestra would play in Baltimore.

"You would have to find someone who died to get a ticket to the Philadelphia Orchestra," Wolfe jokes. "But I loved the principal clarinet player Anthony Gigliotti and I wanted to be an orchestra musician."

Undeterred, when the best team with the best players come to town, and you aspire to one day drive the ball over the centerfield fence in the bottom of the ninth, last game of the world series, you find a way into the game. At the time, the BSO was barely worth the price of admission. A fellow Peabody student-musician working the event propped open the back door of the Lyric and, in a slappy move worthy of hormonal adolescent films, Wolfe and several of his friends would sneak in.

Another of Wolfe's woodwind friends from the summer Pittsburg American Wind Symphony, Frank Ell, a clarinet student at the Curtis Institute of Music in Philadelphia, invited Wolfe to trek north to the City of Brotherly Love and meet Gigliotti whom he studied under.

"I was dedicated to Peabody and I didn't know if it was kosher to do that," said Wolfe, laughing it off. "But I did, I went. I wanted to be an orchestral musician. I'd been studying with Sid since I was in the ninth grade. He was my mentor. He started me on this path, but I'd learned everything he could teach me. So I'd sneak up to Philly and took some lessons from Gigliotti."

Sidney Forrest, never found out. At least that's what Wolfe thinks. It was a gutsy move by a young enterprising musician determined to outrun the inevitable intimate visions of despair, a Nuremberg landscape fragmented by war, a father who cared little for music. "Any orchestra," said Wolfe, "I would've worked for any orchestra."

So, he studied on the sly with Gigliotti.

You may not get the musical results you would from a professional orchestra, but you ought to see the expressions on their faces and the tremendous spontaneity of their enthusiasm when they make music for the first time as performers. You don't get that from a professional orchestra.

—Chris Wolfe on conducting the Baltimore County Youth Orchestra. Quote taken from the *Baltimore Sun*.

Of course it is spring, 1976. There's a strong urge to get out and enjoy the sun as the cold, gray vestiges of winter releases its grip on everything—gloomy moods, flat performances, and new ideas. Chris Wolfe is packing up his clarinet after a Baltimore Symphony Orchestra rehearsal when pianist Arno Drucker, music department head at the then Essex Community College (ECC now CCBC), approaches with a proposition.

Wolfe is more than ten years into a career with the BSO as a clarinetist. The orchestra has been steadily extending its season, but has not yet attained the financial security of a 52-week schedule. The lifestyle of a BSO concert musician in the mid-1970s is still one of balancing the passion and privilege of being compensated for playing music with the distasteful necessity of scrounging for part-time work. The fortunate ones, like Wolfe, could give up delivering papers and selling lingerie door-to-door.

"I was teaching part-time at the preparatory department at Peabody and also at Morgan State University and Goucher College," said Wolfe. "Drucker asked me to take a drive with him, out to Essex Community College, that the school wanted to add an instrumental component to the music department."

Wolfe immediately balked at the idea, first at leaving the agreeable confines of Baltimore City, not wanting to commute out to the "boonies," an ironic twist considering his father's affinity for the verdant hills of pastoral Virginia where Wolfe came-of-age.

"I also didn't even know what a community college was," said Wolfe. "But it didn't sound good. I had the perception of community colleges a lot of parents have now, that it's second rate. I learned nothing could be further from the truth."

Drucker came close to begging and finally Wolfe conceded. They took the drive out to the county, the "boonies," and the campus of ECC. The student population was smaller, more vocational in 1976, the grounds flanked by a small hospital and farms. He met Dean Mike Meyer, Bill Ellis, the division head, and Scott Black, the new drama department head who'd been asked to grow the theater program. The push was to build a comprehensive, recognized arts program.

"I had a full-time job with the BSO and didn't know if I could do it," said Wolfe. "First, I told them, you need a jazz and rock component, and a symphony orchestra. Plus, there were no kids that came here, especially no music students from area high schools."

The challenge seduced Wolfe's self-fixed role as ambassador for instrumental music— the world is better off with more of it—and overpowered his nascent sense of responsibility for teaching, for passing on what was becoming a vast store of knowledge. Wolfe would adjunct for a year, to "see what he could do."

The first thing he did was steal students.

"I had access to a big studio, including what I had at Goucher and Morgan," said Wolfe. "I told all my students, all the kids I had signed up for lessons, to go to Essex the following year. I built a clarinet choir and we performed at a national music educator's conference in Washington D.C. and they were a huge hit."

Essex Community College President, Vic Wanty became a big supporter. Wolfe got money to start a youth orchestra. A year later he became full-time and for 38 years, he excelled in two full-time jobs.

Pianist and ECC Creative Arts Center Director, Carol Kingsmore, in the summer of 1976, attended Harvard Business School's seminar in arts management. With help from grant writers, support from Dean Meyer, and without a steady source of string players from high schools in the immediate vicinity, which somehow determined string sections were too time consuming and diverted students away from English and math, Kingsmore and Wolfe built the Baltimore County Youth Orchestra, 75 students between the ages of 12 and 19. Wolfe just had to reach a little further to convince high school string players in other districts to trek to Essex for rehearsals.

"The orchestra became very popular in a very short period of time," Wolfe said with obvious enthusiasm. "We received a lot of good write-ups in lots of publications. I conducted it for 11 years, and finally it got to be too much. Eventually the BSO took it over, which is really where it belonged."

In 1999, at the age of 57, Wolfe found time to earn a master's degree from Towson University in music education and started teaching courses in music appreciation. Today he spends a lot of time still in his ambassador role, calling on local high schools (which have since added string sections), recruiting musicians for his CCBC classes, and deflating the stigma of community colleges for wary parents and students. Suburbanized tract houses and strip malls have shortened the distance to CCBC Essex from every direction.

The first thing he did was steal students.

It's almost spring, 2018. Wolfe counts more than a dozen auditions since he graduated from Herndon High 60 years ago. Most of them he failed. He never became a full-time conductor, principal clarinetist with a major orchestra, or a music professor at a major conservatory. He survived the most precarious cut however, and has played for and survived the life he worked for. In today's digitally-frenzied, ever-transitory economy, it is harder and harder to realize the self, to fuse it with purpose and "calling," to build not just a career but a life, especially if it is a life invested in the arts and humanities. Wolfe is still learning, still applying, still running, still augmenting his sense of self. It's always spring and there inevitably will be more auditions.

Biography & Documentary: Academia's Evolution
by Billy Tooma

"We are not just a Babel of voices. Nor is the culture that surrounds us."
—Lois W. Banner

History should not be viewed as an artless regurgitation of facts, figures, and dates. The story of humanity should be approached from a more humanistic perspective. The implementation of the study of biography and documentary can build bridges across time, creating connections, thoughts, and opinions among students in ways a standardized, oftentimes sterile, textbook cannot. But the two are, more often than not, viewed as oddities, unfit for classroom use. Academia does not receive them well. Jonathan Haslam writes that biography is, unfortunately, "seen as somewhat eccentric: a whimsical detour from well-travelled direct routes . . . ," but it could not be any further from the truth. Biography is not a quirky genre meant to be seen as an alternative to a mainstream understanding of history. And documentary has suffered from what many films in other genres suffer from: an output of questionable titles of poor production quality. The reluctance to rely on it as a teaching tool

has grown because people tend to focus on the negative results of working within its realm rather than on the positive. Geoffrey C. Ward says that it "really is a terrible shame that there should be any hostility between serious filmmakers and serious historians because the cause of informing the public about the past we all share is a great one" (Bernard and Robin 136-137). It becomes this constant Sisyphus-like struggle to push for the use of documentaries within education. Conservative academics like tangible teaching tools. Documentaries represent an intangible audio/visual experience. This is what they are wary of. Students must be taught to understand that they do not exist within "a vacuum, and [that] the social, political, economic and historical forces" of their times were spawned over millennia by *real* people, not just printed names with birth and death dates next to them in parentheses (Fowler 54). History, if handled via a literary (not to be confused with fictional) experience (in this case through biography and documentary) can stimulate and reinvigorate the learning experience.

Biography embodies years of work. A scholarly paper does not, on average, do the same. Many academics look at the genre as time-consuming. One work produced within a three-year period gets outweighed by several shorter works within that same amount of time. Publish, publish, publish—this is what many conservative academics of today have had ingrained into their minds. Brian Jay Jones says that he is not exactly sure where the disdaining originates from but that perhaps biography is "viewed as navel-gazing" and that "there's also a shaking of the head, too, when . . . [conservative academics] hear that someone is writing a three-volume biography of some Obscure Left-Handed Nearsighted Unappreciated Poet." But no one should be allowed to judge the biographer working on that. Leave that individual alone. Once the work is completed and made available then judge it by its ability to teach. If it succeeds then no one should question its merits.

The low opinion of biography in conservative academia can be linked to the way in which this type of historian tends to think of the genre as second-rate. There is a clear indication of jealously on the conservative historian's part due to biography being relatively more accessible than the works they are producing. Lois W. Banner writes that this type of historian sees biography "as inherently limited because it involves only one life, derives from a belles-lettres tradition rather than a scientific or sociological one" (580). It becomes an "us versus them" mentality on the part of the conservative historian who is forced to compete with authors who may not possess their level of education but who are producing works of value, being read by large audiences, and receiving praise. The belles-lettres tradition

notion points to a mental disconnect many suffer from when viewing biography because, as H. Ramsey Fowler writes, biography "and autobiography are both forms of fiction, and that they deserve to be thought of seriously as literature and to be *taught* in the . . . classroom" (52). So because biography is formed through a much more creative/artistic process the conservative historian balks at its value; many would rather see hard facts presented in such a way that would cause learners to lose interest, or worse, not retain any of the information.

The reluctance to rely on it as a teaching tool has grown because people tend to focus on the negative results of working within its realm rather than on the positive.

Creative forms must be allowed to figure themselves out through trial and error. Nothing is completely defined all at once, and, definitions can change over the course of time. Biography has changed greatly since Plutarch's *Parallel Lives* and so too has documentary changed since the days of Robert J. Flaherty's *Nanook of the North* (1922). Ken Burns admits that "what makes documentary a kind of lesser animal, in the scale of things, is that for too long it was a didactic, essayistic thing; an expression of someone else's already-arrived-at ends, and not interested in narrative" (Cunningham 33). There is this sense of proving the worth of documentaries among filmmakers. At the heart of that, which is the same for biographies, is making sure a *good* story is being told.

Biography must *teach* its readers *something*. It cannot be dry, yet it cannot be a fabrication. The biographer must understand that while they are limited by the concrete facts, they are not bound to those facts in that the storytelling process should read like a government document, or a very well-researched dissertation. David McCullough is quoting E.M. Forster when he says that "If I tell you that the king died and then the queen died, that's a sequence of events. If I tell you that the king died and then the queen died of grief, that's a story," and it proves true to the structure of biography. Nobody wants to open a book and read through a laundry list of information. That is not interesting. But a framework narrative which ties that information together creates a dynamic that entertains and informs without warping what really happened.

The best biographies are the ones which can present the information that the author has accumulated and made approachable for readers. Biography and history should not be viewed as separate areas of study, rather, the former should serve to enhance the latter. Both are "based on archival research, [which] interweaves historical categories and methodologies, reflects current political and theoretical concerns, and raises complex issues of truth and proof" (Banner 580). It ends up being entirely in the presentation of the material.

Biographers may step away from their subjects but they never fully divorce them.

The biographer, by forming a coherent, honest story based on primary source material is going to outperform the historian by generating an accessible style of prose. If anything, biography should challenge the conservative historian to deliver their scholarship in a more creative way.

Documentary, regardless of the subjects being covered, should work in a similar way. There needs to be a deep narrative constructed in order for the filmmaker to convey their message to viewers. Burns points out that the "medium is so richly panned for being superficial. And in many cases that's a deserved thing . . ." (Cunningham 33). He is speaking out against those who construct an entire story on paper, film it, and call it a day. There is a coldness to that approach, which translates to the screen, and ultimately turns audiences and critics off. The same approach to biography is the same to documentary even when the latter is not biographical: the accessibility of the subject matter, not dumbed down, but not ivory tower, rather, a mixture of fact and an entertaining presentation.

The responsibility of the documentary filmmaker is to understand that what they are creating "is intimately tied to historical memory. Not only does it seek to reconstruct historical narrative, but it often functions as an historical document itself" (Rabinowitz 119). So the filmmaker takes on the responsibility of doing right by their subjects in order to present their stories. The audience is not ignorant. Many who come to a certain documentary are bringing their preconceived notions and ideas. The filmmaker's duty is to ensure that if they are going to challenge said preconceptions then there is evidence to back up their decisions because the work "calls upon its audience to participate in historical remembrance by presenting an intimate view of reality" (Rabinowitz 119). If there is new information being brought to light that could perhaps paint the subject in a different, not even necessarily negative, way then the filmmaker needs to be aware that their audience's acceptance of this new construct is imperative.

The shortsightedness of many conservative scholars comes from resentment rooted in their own education. Biography is *specific*, not *broad*. It can cover the lifespan of a person, but that number of years is unlikely going to get close to and exceed one hundred. History classes—general ones, surveys, etc.—go well beyond the times of any one individual. So biography goes against the curriculum that exudes what is considered "well-roundedness." It trumps the conservative academic's view that history needs to be studied a certain way. Jones believes that the accessibility of biography lends itself the audience which the academics simply do

not have. He says that "I have no idea how a telephone works . . . . I would never buy or read a book with the schematics of the phone . . . . But I sure would like reading about Alexander Graham Bell trying to figure it all out," which, by doing so, Jones feels he would grow to appreciate the device that much more. It is the focus on individuals, even specific *things*, which guide people towards biography as well as the characterization of those who lived through the events and happenings.

Biographers are all too often accused of being flash-in-the-pan experts on their subjects, leaving them behind once the project has been completed with the next one on the horizon.

Nothing can be further from the truth. Biographers, especially those who do not dedicate themselves to one specific person, place, or thing (which is what many conservative historians end up doing), must become deeply immersed in the time and place their subjects lived in. They are "detectives and interpreters, attempting to illuminate the past and to inter-weave its threads in new and compelling patterns . . . . A life span of seventy years, after all, encompasses nearly a century of historical development" (Banner 582). Biographers and historians are not unlike one another, so the divide amongst them is ridiculous. Being able to pick out key pieces of information that have never been looked at or have been looked at in only one way is what both sides end up doing in order to produce their work, and sometimes it leads them to more projects. McCullough became so entrenched in the life of John Adams and the 18th century that he had enough leftover research material to write *1776* (2005). Biographers may step away from their subjects but they never fully divorce them. Those who criticize them must come to understand that the desire to tell stories is what drives them to go from subject to subject.

Information, presented in a classroom at any level, is all too often watered down. Students do not feel connected to anything. This causes them to not care. When Ward says that "history

is biography—what interests people is what happened to other people" (Bernard and Robin 135), he is emphasizing the importance of not glossing over the fact that the stories being told are about *people*. He further states that history "is just dates and movements if you don't have some individuals to hold on to" (Bernard and Robin 135), which strengthens what Jones said above: no one wants to learn cold facts without a reason to *care*. If anything, above all else, what separates humanity from the rest of the animal kingdom it is that we tell stories. Whether they are fact or fiction depends on taste.

It is that personalized connection that the stories told in documentaries are trying to generate. Students, at all levels, are trying to form better understandings of the times they sprung from, currently are living in, and the ones they hope to have a hand in forming. Arch A. Mercey was talking about the importance of incorporating documentary films into the classroom as far back as 1939 when he wrote that books alone could never give students the type

of experience films could because by bringing the latter into the mix "the teacher is taking his class on a field trip to every corner of the earth and the teacher can in fact dramatize problems of the social sciences in his own area through the use of the camera" (308). Nearly eighty years later the same philosophies are being fought for where the study of documentary is concerned. To watch a film is to see it, feel it, internalize it, and react to it. When Arthur H. Auerbach began using documentaries as part of his grade school curriculum he was careful to ensure that discussions immediately followed a screening because "these provided not only focused review on the specific topic but also tapped into the students' emotional response" (518). The textbook is too often skimmed in order to memorize what may or may not be on a test. Students are cheated out of developing an in-depth knowledge base. By using documentary as a teaching tool the students become active participants because the audio/visual experience enriches their previously abstract notion of historical, even contemporary, events.

The characters of history must be the ones telling the story, even in a biography of a nonperson. In McCullough's *The Path Between the Seas: The Creation of the Panama Canal, 1870-1914* (1977) the story is told from the perspective of those who were involved with the construction, from the politicians who pushed for it to the laypeople who physically brought it into existence. McCullough says that history "is best understood as an unfolding story. I think there's more intellectual honesty in seeing it that way, from *within* what happened." Readers develop a rapport this way. It is a bond that cannot be formed when reading a textbook. There is no humanization going on.

To watch a film is to see it, feel it, internalize it, and react to it.

Just as biography brings vibrancy to the written word so too can documentary bring it to the screen. But it must also adhere to what is most important and that is to be lively. Burns considers himself "an emotional archaeologist, uninterested in the dry dates and facts of the past" (Cunningham 21), which speaks to his need to not fail his audience. People, a lot of the time, do not know what they want. Sometimes they have to be told, but not in a forceful way. Interest in the Civil War grew because of Burns' documentary on it. In that film he had to gather voices from all across the splintered nation. But he knew that "you cannot manipulate character development to fit into the arc of your narrative, but at the same time, the character development is a given because you know what happens to that person" (Cunningham 35). Audiences sitting down to watch his documentary knew the Confederacy was going to lose, but it was the journey, via the various voices, which kept them fixated.

The interdisciplinary nature of documentaries (and by extension, biographies) challenges the conservative academic to admit that fields of study are not isolated islands. They should begin to comprehend that documentary films "have made important gestures and interventions into both public and private history . . . . Documentary then is historical filmmaking; but documentary crosses a number of disciplinary divides: anthropology for one" (Rabinowitz 123). The textbooks put in students' laps do not provide them with a full understanding of the ramifications of historical events beyond what publishers have determined to be relevant. They will learn that Thomas Jefferson wrote the Declaration of Independence and was the third president of the United States of America, but watching Burns' film on the founding father will make them aware of Jefferson having lived the end of his life in debt and bankruptcy, and reading Annette Gordon-Reed's *The Hemingses of Monticello: An American Family* (2008) will show students that the whitewashing of history has sadly been, and continues to be, widespread.

A question arises out of this need to understand what has come before us: are we getting the entire story? The short answer is no. The longer answer, according to Joseph Epstein, deals with the fact "that even the most superior biography cannot be complete. Biographies may be authorized; they can even be impressively authoritative; but they are never, ultimately, definitive." Jones' *Washington Irving* (2008) boasts on its cover that it is "The Definitive Biography of America's First Bestselling Author." The author says that he "*hates* that subtitle" as he always thought his subject should have been advertised as "An American Original." When asked the question of definitive versus representational, Jones' answer was: "Can a biography be definitive? Boy, you've got me. Until people stop being so . . . wonderfully inscrutable, probably not. Sorry, disappointing answer, I know." His response is not a disappointment; actually, it strengthens the fact that biographers are never going to know every exact detailed moment of their subjects' lives, so they have to research and discover what they can.

It becomes a combination of consciously and subconsciously deciding what goes into the telling of a life, be it someone else's or the author's own. Conclusive and concise is what the conservative historian wants. They want to know when one war ended and another began or when one emperor's reign was cut short by a coup. But biography works differently because it is working less towards conclusive and more towards what is most *accurate*. Fowler points out that neither Plutarch nor Thomas Carlyle intended to write what he calls chronicles.

People want to learn. People want to be entertained. They should be allowed to do those two simultaneously.

Instead, he writes that they "were writing interpretations that were meant to isolate, to crystallize, and to immortalize great fortune, great genius, great talent, or even great folly . . . . [They] were searching for the essential truth of each life portrayed" (52). Falsities have no place in biography or history, yet the former tends to brave with treading those waters because the biographers recognize the importance of being able to, like a writer of fiction, select, emphasize, condense, and arrange materials, knowing they must stay true to the information that has been gathered (Fowler 52).

Ward says the same where documentary is concerned: "Nobody making a film is ever trying to make a definitive anything. No book is definitive, and certainly no film can be" (Bernard and Robin 136). Even though the documentaries made from his screenplays have runtimes of eleven, fourteen, and twenty-three hours in length, none are the *definitive* versions

of the War Between the States, the Roosevelts, and the National Pastime, respectively. And this is what brings people back to biography, especially when there are multiple retellings of the same life.

The very idea that any one biography or documentary could tell the *entire* story is ridiculous. A married couple might be together for over fifty years and still not know one another entirely. Burns sees the major task of constructing biographical documentaries as "a failing enterprise—because we don't even know the people closest to us, our family members, our loved ones. It's impossible to know anybody. But the effort is what propels the human adventure . . ." (Cunningham 32). He is not damning those who tell the stories of others or the histories of places, things, and events, rather, he is saying this is why it should never stop. Burns' films are not the only ones to look at the subjects covered. Go into any library or bookstore and numerous biographies on, say, Napoleon Bonaparte, are there. People want to learn. People want to be entertained. They should be allowed to do those two simultaneously.

Biography, in all of its forms, has become quite popular, particularly in the United States. There is this desire to take in the life of another, learn from them, and feel connected to the subject. Biography "at its best is a good read, and the older one gets, the more attractive and entertaining biography becomes" (Haslam), which signifies something important: a rebellion against education. Adolescents are not checking out or buying biographies in droves because they are still suffering under a flawed system of instruction. It is taking people longer to find themselves attracted to the genre of biography. This is key. Something within them realizes this is how they should learn. They think that they have to be older to be able to appreciate the stories of other peoples' experiences. They do not realize that feeling is

unfounded: they can understand, to one degree or another, life's complexities at any age. This approach can be brought back to the younger generation if they were only allowed time away from the current curriculum wrapped around textbooks.

Readers of biography must also be aware that their fascination with the genre stems from a yearning to comprehend the people who shaped the world. Biographies "remind us that in the end men and women, not impersonal forces, are the true measure and motor force of history" (Epstein), which reinforces the personal connection. We tend to put historical figures on pedestals, especially when the conservative scholars favor them, and forget that they were born, lived, and died just like every other human to grace the face of the earth. What biography does is humanize those who have been deified. That is the difference between a textbook and a biography: the latter challenges the sterile nature of the former.

There is a rich age of documentary film-making coming into being. This surge in the medium has lent credence to those who believe in the work they are doing. Sean O'Hagan writes that we "are living in a moment when film-makers, the young filmmakers in particular, are increasingly turning towards documentary as a way to make sense of the world they live in," and Burns was a catalyst for that. Today's documentarians grew up watching his work on PBS. The interest his films generate in the subjects he covers is remarkable. The budding filmmaker of today is going to know that the medium can make a difference on many levels. SeaWorld no longer holds orca shows thanks to the backlash they received from *Blackfish* (2013). Sixto Rodriguez, obscure everywhere except South African and Australia, is now in his 70s and touring worldwide because of *Searching for Sugar Man* (2012).

None of this would have been possible twenty years ago. Film stock is very expensive, but, according to David Edelstein, "it wasn't until the advent of small digital cameras that the line between video and celluloid began to blur." Yet, not everyone can pick up a camera

and shoot a good documentary. People often make this mistake that because the technology is accessible, anyone can be successful with it. That could not be any further from the truth. Ward says that a "good many academic historians are basically suspicious of the medium and want to blame you for the sins of all the other people who have made films" (Bernard and Robin 136). When making a documentary one needs to be disciplined and know, at minimum, the basics of camera operation, sound, and lighting. The overall goal is to give life to something that will reach people on an emotional level and that cannot be accomplished by fumbling around with equipment and various types of editing and rendering software.

This aforementioned rich age is only just beginning. The goal of a filmmaker ten years ago was to make a film, get it into some sort of film festival, and, the cinematic gods willing, sign a DVD distribution deal. It was a singular road towards getting your work made available. That,

however, is no longer the case. Edelstein writes that "there are so many outlets for exhibition—not just via commercial releases but in festivals, on cable, via video on demand, and over the Internet," which highlights the now seemingly endless avenues towards exposure. Anyone can now make their documentary available on DVD via Amazon; the goal for many is to now get a deal signed where the streaming rights are concerned. And even the avenue of streaming can be a most liberating experience. Times change. People change. Sean Dunne, someone who makes documentary films but who has a career outside of that to sustain himself, says, "I want to put this [his body of work] on the Internet today for free and say, 'Here. Let's talk about this,'" (qtd. in Edelstein). He wants to be a part of the conversation. He wants people to watch his work. He wants them to connect to the individuals whose stories are being told.

In 2010 a group of likeminded biographers came together in order to form the Biographers

International Organization (BIO). Among the goals of the founding members was the one which called for the encouragement of public interest in and appreciation for biography. Over the six years of its existence BIO has grown to well over one hundred members, holding an annual conference where they can converge for a few days in order to report on the state of biography as they see it. At the second annual conference then president Nigel Hamilton said that by confronting the challenges biography faces "together, rather than singly, we can ensure the survival of biography as seriously researched, articulately composed, and well-produced work chronicling the lives of real individuals: a craft that has been in existence since Greek and Roman times." When individuals with similar goals come together like this then that means one door is about to close as another begins to open. BIO is ready, willing, and able, to advocate for biography as a way in which to alter the conservative approach to history instruction.

Documentary film festivals, both domestic and international, are all over the map. What began as a category in one film festival or another has branched out and become its own thing. When a movement can take on a life of its own then the message is obvious: the objectives of said movement cannot be ignored. The backbone of this is the International Documentary Association (IDA), founded in 1982, and now boasting some two-thousand members from fifty-three countries. IDA, like BIO, advocates heavily for its medium and the filmmakers who work within it. Its members describe themselves as being part of a documentary culture, which exemplifies their strong-willed feelings towards their craft.

Students want to be entertained when they are learning. This is entirely possible. But it cannot be accomplished through using a stand-ardized textbook. They will suffer under the system of banking education that Paulo Freire criticized. Students, by studying biography, "emotionally identify with the texts they are reading and with the professors teaching them, thus engaging in a personally transformative process as they reflect . . . on their own lives

A greater impact is made, a deeper footprint formed, and history becomes more than a summary of thousands of years within just several hundred pages.

and the pasts and present in which they are living" (Banner 585-586). If they are given the opportunity to see the stories through documentaries they are being educated through an audio/visual approach, taking in the information as they see it on the screen, seeing and hearing primary and secondary sources come alive. A greater impact is made, a deeper footprint formed, and history becomes more than a summary of thousands of years within just several hundred pages. The study of biography and documentary can no longer afford to be marginalized. Both must be embraced if the modern-day conservative academic approach to history instruction is to evolve for the better.

Bibliography

Appiah, Kwame Anthony, and Henry Louis Gates. *Africana: The Encyclopedia of the African and African American Experience*. Oxford University Press, 1999.

Auerbach, Arthur H. "Teaching Diversity: Using a Multifaceted Approach to Engage Students." *PS: Political Science and Politics*, vol. 45, no. 3, 2012, pp. 516-520.

Banner, Lois W. "Biography as Literature." *The Sewanee Review*, vol. 100, no. 3, 1992, pp. 382-396.

Bernard, Shelia Curran. "Documentary Storytelling: The Drama of Real Life." *Writers Store*, www.writerstore.com/documentary-storytelling-the-drama-of-real-life/. Accessed 9 Feb. 2016.

Bernard, Shelia Curran, and Ken Robin. *Archival Storytelling: A Filmmaker's Guide to Finding, Using, and Licensing Third-Party Visuals and Music*. Focal Press, 2009.

Biographers International Organization. BIO, www.biographersinternational.org/. Accessed 3 Jan. 2017.

The Black Eagle of Harlem. Directed by Billy Tooma, Icon Independent Films, 2017.

Blackfish. Directed by Gabriela Cowperthwaite, CNN Films, 2013.

Chamberlin, Clarence D. *Record Flights*. Dorrance & Company, 1928.

Cirilo, Anthony. "Anthony Cirilo Talks About Poetry of Witness." Interview by Loren Kleinman. *The Huffington Post*, 14 Dec. 2015, www.huffingtonpost.com/loren-kleinman/anthony-cirilo-talks-abou_b_8800642.html. Accessed 2 Jan. 2017.

The Civil War. Directed by Ken Burns, Florentine Films, 1990.

Cunningham, Megan. *The Art of Documentary: Fifteen Conversations with Leading Directors, Cinematographers, Editors, and Producers*. 2nd ed., New Riders, 2014. 29

Edelstein, David. "Edelstein: How Documentary Became the Most Exciting Kind of Filmmaking." *Vulture*, www.vulture.com/2013/04/edelstein-documentary-is-better-than-filmmaking.html. Accessed 11 Feb. 2016.

Epstein, Joseph. "The Art of Biography." *The Wall Street Journal*, www.wsj.com/articles/the- art-of-biography-1451514816. Accessed 2 Feb. 2016.

Clarence Chamberlin: Fly First & Fight Afterward. Directed by Billy Tooma, Icon Independent Films, 2011.

Flyers in Search of a Dream. Produced by Philip S. Hart, PBS, 1987.

Fowler, H. Ramsey. "Eldridge Cleaver, Daniel Berrigan, and the Teaching of Biography as Literature." *Interpretations*, vol. 4, no. 1, 1972, pp. 52-62.

Franklin, Guy E. *Hubert Fauntleroy Julian: The Rest of the Story, Harlem's Black Eagle*. Amazon Kindle Direct Publishing, 2014.

Freire, Paulo. *Pedagogy of the Oppressed*. Continuum, 1970.

Gordon-Reed, Annette. *The Hemingses of Monticello: An American Family*. W. W. Norton & Company, 2008.

Gruesser, John Cullen. *Black on Black: Twentieth-Century African American Writing about Africa*. The University Press of Kentucky, 2000.

Hart, Philip S. *Flying Free: America's First Black Aviators*. Simon & Schuster, 1996.

Haslam, Jonathan. "Biography and its importance to history." *Winter Conference*, winterconference.history.ac.uk/2012/10/16/biography-and-its-importance-to-history/. Accessed 1 Feb. 2016.

International Documentary Association. IDA, www.documentary.org. Accessed 3 Jan. 2017

Jones, Brian Jay. *Jim Henson: The Biography*. Ballantine Books, 2013. 30

    Washington Iriving: The Definitive Biography of America's First Bestselling Author. Arcade Publishing, 2011.

Jones, Brian Jay. Personal interview. 12 Feb. 2016.

Julian, Hubert, and John Bulloch. *Black Eagle*. The Adventurers Club, 1964.

Mercey, Arch A. "Teaching Social Studies through Documentary Films." *The Journal of Higher Education*, vol. 10, no. 6, 1939, pp. 303-308.

McCullough, David. "David McCullough, The Art of Biography No. 2." Interview by Elizabeth Gaffney and Benjamin Ryder Howe. *The Paris Review*, Fall 1999, www.theparisreview.org/interviews/894/the-art-of-biography-no-2-david-mccullough. Accessed 9 Feb. 2016.

McCullough, David. "History and Knowing Who We Are." *American Heritage*, www.americanheritage.com/content/history-and-knowing-who-we-are. Accessed 2. Jan. 2017.

1776. Simon & Schuster, 2005.

The Johnstown Flood. Simon & Schuster, 1968.

The Path Between the Seas: The Creation of the Panama Canal, 1870–1914. Simon & Schuster, 1977.

Nanook of the North. Directed by Robert J. Flaherty, Pathé Exchange, 1922.

Nugent, John Peer. *The Black Eagle*. Bantam Books, 1971.

O'Hagan, Sean. "Camera, laptop, action: the new golden age of documentary." *The Guardian*, www.theguardian.com/film/2010/nov/07/documentary-digitial-revolution-sean-ohagan. Accessed 11 Feb. 2016.

Poetry of Witness. Directed by Billy Tooma and Anthony Cirilo, Icon Independent Films, 2015. 31

Rabinowitz, Paula. "Wreckage and Wreckage: History, Documentary and the Ruins of Memory." *History and Theory*, vol. 32, no. 2, 1993, pp. 119-137.

Searching for Sugar Man. Directed by Malik Bendjelloul, Red Box Film, 2012.

Shaftel, David. "The Black Eagle of Harlem." *Air & Space Magazine*, www.airspacemag.com/history-of-flight/the-black-eagle-of-harlem-95208344/. Accessed 23 Dec. 2015.

Thomas Jefferson. Directed by Ken Burns, Florentine Films, 1997.

The Goddess Lakshmi.

A New School of Feminism: An Academic Exercise or an Ethnographic Reality?
by Sunithi Gnanadoss

As a first-generation Indian immigrant in the '90s, reading and teaching feminist literature in an American classroom proved to be a far cry from the school back home. A cultural voice that did not naturally align with the likes of Virginia Woolf, Betty Friedan, and Gloria Steinem was now changing the default harmony of its score in this new environment. There was an evolution from the initial paradigm of compliance and its coercive power of dharma, otherwise defined as duty to a set role, to a new non-dharma paradigm of emancipation. A new canvas was emerging. The distinct paint tubes of karma and caste were not sold in this market. There was a crying need to deliver to an emerging audience with calls for new pedagogy.

As time went on, the ethnographer in me saw profound differences. I was looking at my unfamiliar home with a new lens, and looking at my old home with a new lens as well—the intersecting world was baffling, exciting, and yet alienating. For all the flaws that my old home culture contained, the familiarity of tradition contradicted the new world. Alas! I could relate to the

first generation immigrant women characters in fiction; I recognized the nuanced language of assimilation, emancipation and dilemma. Thus, began my PhD research on Indian feminism as both a pedant and an ethnographer. I found myself operating from a hole in the theoretical volume of feminism; the existing theories needed a new classification—The Indian Immigrant Woman. The home culture, the new culture, the assimilation or non-assimilation, produced a woman who asked:

> We were born to one of the world's oldest civilizations—five thousand years old—and we emigrated to one of the youngest. Which values and customs are superior: those of our birthplace or those of the land where we chose to settle? What to adopt? What to reject? What to discard?
>
> (Pradhan 102)

Marxian feminism framed the discussion that economic freedom was feminist emancipation. This is echoed in the second wave of feminism. But Marxian feminism was really not freedom for the traditional Indian woman who had to wade through several millennia of coercive traditions and beliefs. The Multicultural School of Feminism, as its label suggests, was too broad for specific and authentic interpretation; The Intersectional Feminism of race, gender and culture had too many cross-currents to fit the framework for authentically interpreting the Indian Immigrant woman. Did the story of the minority Indian woman immigrant cross paths with the minority African American woman whose past involved slavery? An honest answer would be no; to marry the two groups seemed to me to be a slap in the face of diverse historical paths that, in turn, produced different scenarios. What about the post-colonial voice of Gayatri Spivak, who said that the British were culpable for the subaltern voice of the Indian woman through the palimpsestic history that colonization produced? Did the British institute theories of caste, karma and dharma? The answer is no.

Hence, if this tradition pre-dated colonization and continued its embedded norms in post colonized India, the honest argument goes beyond post-colonial considerations. While I am not dispensing the dragnet of colonial plunder of Indian geopolitics, my premise is that in the case of the Indian woman, colonization is not culpable for the strong subaltern phenomena among traditional Indian woman. She was too far hidden in the wings from the main stage of colonialism, and thus, the traditional Indian woman deserves an examination of her status and her history.

In my dissertation, "Theorizing Indo-Immigrant Feminism: A Study of Indo-Immigrant Novels," I assert a new school of feminism. It is here that I give the Indian Immigrant Woman a voice. What follows here is some historical and cultural context as well as some examples illuminated in my work.

The pre-colonial idealized state of the Indian woman is best seen in the label, Sumangali. This label is interchangeable with Goddess Lakshmi. This sumangali, with the right karma, is the goddess of good fortune who keeps a home prosperous. A married woman/sumangali has the most privileged position both individually and collectively in Indian society. Her good karma results in the husband being alive, and her home being successful. But when karma takes a wrong turn, then the Sumangali or Goddess status is stripped from the woman. And like her ancestors, she is encouraged to commit sati—the act of dying in the funeral pyre of the husband, or in less antiquated times, fit the non-personhood mould. Ironically, sati was banned by the British. But the

Her good karma results in the husband being alive, and her home being successful. But when karma takes a wrong turn, then the Sumangali or Goddess status is stripped from the woman.

fear of not being a sumangali is insidious in the subcontinent among traditional Indian women who follow the tenets of customs and beliefs that date back to the *Laws of Manu*, to *The Mahabharata*, and to *The Ramayana*.

Festivals like Diwali celebrate the return of the abducted Sita whose role and character in *The Ramayana* acts as an embodiment of the ideal woman. Sita follows Rama into exile; Sita disobeys Rama when she steps out of the house to feed a stranger; Sita is abducted by the stranger and a war ensues showing a devoted Rama in pursuit of his wife. The happy ending has a twist when the suspicion of Rama is aroused about Sita's chastity. Sita is willing to walk on live coals to prove her innocence. This ritual is referred to as Agni-Pariksha. While one is drawn into the mutual love of the couple, one is also disturbed by the ritual. During Diwali, the Goddess Lakshmi is invited to bless the home and the Sumangali status is deified and idealized, and the parameters clearly drawn for the traditional Indian women.

Another ritual/celebration is Karwa Chauth. Here the sumangali fasts and prays for the longevity of a husband and for his wellbeing. This is part of India's cultural landscape and fiction that reflects traditional realities. This uninterrupted norm goes back to the Laws of Manu:

> Though destitute of virtue, or seeking pleasure elsewhere, or devoid of good qualities, (yet) a husband must be constantly worshipped as a god by a faithful wife. 155. No sacrifice, no vow, no fast must be performed by women apart from their husbands; if a wife obeys her husband, she will for that (reason alone) be exalted in heaven. 156. A faithful wife, who desires to dwell (after death) with her husband, must never do anything that might displease him who took her hand, whether he be alive or dead.
> (*The Laws of Manu* 34)

This is seen in the novel, *That Long Silence*. The fasting and prayers for the husband are evident. "If it wasn't her Saturday, it was her Monday or Thursday. Mukta, Jaya's neighbor, had more days of fast that when she could eat a normal meal" (Deshpande 67). Jaya is reminded before her marriage, "Remember a husband is like a sheltering tree . . . without the tree you are dangerously unprotected and vulnerable . . . and so you have to keep the tree alive and flourishing . . . ." (Deshpande 32).

Another example of Sumangali and widowhood is the 2005 movie, *Water*, directed by Deepa Mehta. In the opening scene of the movie, a father asks his eight-year old daughter,

Chuyia, "Child. Do you remember getting married? Your husband is dead. You're a widow now." Soon after, Chuyia is unceremoniously removed from her home and taken to Varanasi, an ashram for widows. In the ashram, one sees the traumatized Chuyia screaming as she tries to run away. Her crime was karma, fate and gender; it was a crime she had not committed, but it was her state of being rather than the consequences of bad action or her own doing. In the light of such norms, is Karwa Chauth a festive veneer for a deep seeded phobia of widowhood, while venerating the state of "sumangali" or married woman status? To make a point, one sees that the Indian husband does not perform any ritual for his wife's wellbeing. This one sided reverence for the male and husband is insidious.

But what about the scene in *The Mahabharata* that involves a wife who has been pawned in a bet? The rivalry in the ancient Kuru kingdom between the Pandavas and the Kauravas leads to the Kauravas challenging their cousins to a gambling game for the kingdom. The Kauravas hosts this gambling game knowing that Yudhishthira, the oldest Pandava sibling, has a weakness for gambling.

In the opening scene of the movie, a father asks his eight-year old daughter, Chuyia, "Child. Do you remember getting married? Your husband is dead. You're a widow now."

The game is rigged and Yudhisthira keeps losing. Every time he loses, he bets away part of his treasury, and then he commits the unthinkable: he bets his wife. Draupadi who is at the palace and is unaware of this turn of events is rudely summoned to the courts. She reminds the summoner that she has her monthly period, and therefore, by tradition, she is staying away as she is considered unclean. Draupadi's

The Disrobing of Draupadi, a miniature of the Basohli School, attributed to Nainsukh, c.1765.

petition is ignored, and she is dragged into the courts by her hair without being given a chance to dress appropriately. In the palace, Draupadi is angered and raises her voice as she repeatedly questions the legal right of Yudhishthira to place her at stake when he had lost himself, and therefore, his freedom and his rights. Draupadi's strong feminist voice of reason is met with taunts and vulgarity, and her cries for mercy fill the halls of the Kuru palace:

> . . . Menstruating, tormented, and trembling with blood flowing, and wearing but one garment, I was dragged into the assembly of the Kurus. In the assembly, in the middle of the Kings, those evil-minded descendants of Dhritarashtra looked upon me, still menstruating, and laughed. While the Pandavas . . . were still alive, those Kauravas, Madhusudana, desired to enjoy me like a serving wench . . . . (qtd

in "Sita and Draupadi: Aggressive Behavior and Female Role Models in the Sanskrit Epics" 67)

Draupadi's Cheer-Haran, literally meaning stripping of one's clothes, marks a definitive moment in the story of *The Mahabharata*. Draupadi is reminded that she is the property of man; Draupadi is the subaltern voice of a woman seeking justice.

This begs the question: is Draupadi's problem just the cult of domesticity?

What about Karma? What about fate and rebirth? What about Dharma? What about religious norms and code of ethics and duty? Can a room of one's own or economic freedom fully answer the traditional Indian woman's struggle? Does rebirth and dharma become more hurdles to cross for the Draupadis who leave India and come to the West? Does this new Draupadi face the anomie of alienation that the sociologist Emile Durkheim alludes to?

If the traditional Indian woman belongs to a paradigm of distinct social norms and taboos, will her immigration to a new paradigm and her evolution feel like deviance?

Theorist Judith Butler references gender constructs as norms that are held in place "by social sanction and taboo" (271). Will the traditional Indian woman who moves to the west carry with her the root culture of social sanction and taboo? The idealized married Indian woman, Sumangali, is the Goddess Lakshmi, the goddess of fortune. What happens to this Indian woman if her good fortune takes a wrong turn; what happens if there is death, loss of wealth, loss of health, does her karma or her fate become her manacle? If Sita and Goddess

In the mind of the Indian Immigrant, the conflict is between her old persona and her new persona.

Lakshmi are the Indian woman's idealized state, what happens if she adopts a western individualism, will she face the consequence of social sanction and taboo? After all, Draupadi was disrobed of choice and voice in the cheer-haran scene thus forming a caveat to Indian women who challenge patriarchy.

The archetypal Indian woman's canvas is different from others; she is manufactured from the threads and prints of antiquity. She is from the unending saree of Draupadi, the ornateness and bounty of Goddess Lakshmi, and the footprints of Sita's feet following Rama into exile.

To have a discussion of society in terms of its parts and influences, it is pertinent to examine what sociologists say about society and culture. "The Social Construction of Reality Theory" states that society is a product created by humans; it is an objective reality, and man is a social product. The traditional paradigm of India with its dominant Hindu Culture

has been the collective conscious of Indian society for centuries. Investigating Durkheim's theory of social construction and social facts can give one the new analyst scholastic tools to examine collective behavior versus individualistic behavior.

Using Émile Durkheim tenets from *The Rules of Sociological Method*, one can ask: What happens to the traditional Indian woman's social fact of constraint while she is at the same time existing in her newly found independence?

Sociology best explains what happens to the traditional Indian women as they step into a new paradigm. One can comprehend this when one observes her social facts. Social facts can be defined as patterns of behavior that are capable of exercising some coercive power upon individuals. For example, the distinct Indian patriarchy assumes power over the woman and the woman is coerced into submission. So when a paradigm shift is experienced, does the new paradigm seem like deviance from traditional and known norms? Does this lead to confusion and anomie?

The Sociological Encyclopedia Britannica defines anomie as, ". . . a condition of instability resulting from a breakdown of standards and values or from a lack of purpose or ideals." Is the confusion a result of double-consciousness? *Double-consciousness* is a concept in social philosophy referring, originally, to a source of inward "twoness" putatively experienced by African-Americans because of their racialized oppression and dis-evaluation in a white-dominated society (Pitman). The concept is often associated with William Edward Burghardt Du Bois (Pitman). The difference is that the Indian woman has a double-consciousness not imposed by the west but by her own cultural paradigm. Therefore, the conflict with the Sitas moving to the United States is not internal versus a hostile external community, but internal consciousness of tradition versus external freedoms of independence. In the mind of the Indian Immigrant, the conflict is between her old persona and her new persona.

We can see this in the female protagonist of Mukherjee's novel, *Jasmine*, when Jyothi becomes Jasmine, Jasmine becomes Jase, and Jase becomes Jane. It is a metaphorical metamorphoses of personality changes, but will the social sanctions and taboos of her past that stalk Jasmine throughout the narrative let go off her? Consider the following lines:

> I cry into Taylor's shoulder, cry through all the lives I've given birth to, cry for all my dead. Then there is nothing I can do. Time will tell if I am a tornado, rubble-maker arising from nowhere and disappearing into a cloud. I am out the door and in the potholed and rutted driveway, scrambling ahead of Taylor, greedy with wants and reckless from hope. (Mukherjee 241)

Her assimilation is not a reflection of structural immigration but of complex immigration integration that is dominated by the anomie of a new paradigm. Her American Dream is challenged by intrinsic hurdles and not extrinsic ones.

When the Indian woman immigrant, who is dominated by caste, karma, dharma, and patriarchy is transplanted into the western cultural soil of individualism, the archetypal psyche of Sita, Draupadi, and Laxmi threaten the peace and prosperity of her Indian home. While her Sita psyche calls for penance, as seen in some characters of Indian immigrant fiction, her break away feminist persona screams for a purging of her "archetypal guilt." Her seemingly antagonistic deci-

sions are seen as the victimizer of the home which is both a paradox of empowerment and alienation.

This prism cannot be explained through the broad schools of Post Colonialism, Marxian Feminism, Intersectional Feminism, Multicultural Feminism or other schools. The individualistic society that the traditional Indian woman confronts in her new environment holds the complex metaphor of a saree and a bikini. Emancipation, to her, may seem as naked and unbecoming. She is a woman without a frame in a museum. I want a frame for her. I want her to be seen, heard studied, honored, and understood.

Editor's note: *Sunithi Gnanadoss will be defending her dissertation this summer (2018) in India at the University of Madras.*

Bibliography

"Anomie." *Encyclopedia Britannica. Encyclopedia Britannica Online.* Encyclopedia Britannica Inc., www.britannica.com/topic/anomie. Accessed Jan 2016.

Behtash Esmail and Fatemeh Sajjadi. "Literary Feminism in India" Journal of Subcontinent Researches. University of Sistan and Baluchestan, Vol 4.No 11, summer 2012 pp.107-117. http://journals.usb.ac.ir/article_840_38da9283a1272971a9c72e64ca4fc6ee.pdf Accessed Jan 2016.

Bumiller, Elizabeth. *May You Be the Mother of a Hundred Sons.* NY: Penguin, 1992.

Butler, Judith. "Performative Acts and Gender Constitution: An Essay in Phenomenology and Feminist Theory." *Theatre Journal* .Vol 40. No.4.pp519-531. Baltimore: Johns Hopkins UP, 1990. www.amherst.edu/system/files/media/1650/butler_performative_acts.pdf

Das, Gurucharan. *The Difficulty of Being Good: On the Subtle Art of Dharma.* NY: Penguin Books, 2009.

Deshpande, Sashi. *That Long Silence.* Penguin, 1989.

Divakurani, Chitra Banerjee. *Palace of Illusions.* First Anchor Books, 2009.

Doniger, Wendy. *The Hindus: An Alternative History.* NY: Penguin, 2009.

Doniger, Wendy. "Mahabharata" *Encylopedia Britannica,* 2015.

Durkheim, E. *Sociology and Philosophy.* New York: The Free Press, 1953.

Durkheim, E. *Suicide: A Study in Sociology.* (J. Spaulding, & G. Simpson, Trans.) New York: The Free Press, 1951.

Elwell, Frank W. "Emile Durkheim on Anomie" *Sociocultural Systems: Principles of Structure and Change.* AU: Press, 2013.

"Karwa Chauth" *Faith, Black Country. BBC. 2014.* www.bbc.co.uk/blackcountry/content/articles/2008/10/20/karwa_chauth_feature.shtml Accessed January 2016.

"Karwa Chauth" *World Heritage.* http://community.worldheritage.org/articles/eng/Karva_Chauth Accessed January 2016.

"Kuru Kingdom in India" *Mysterious History.* http://historycollected.blogspot.com/2013/06/kuru-kingdom-in-india.html#!/2013/06/kuru-kingdom-in-india.html

Lorde, Audre. *Sister Outsider: Essays and Speeches.* Berkeley: Crossing Press.

Lyon, Sarah. "Evaluating Fair Trade Consumption: Politics, Defetishization and Producer Participation." Academia.edu - www.academia.edu/2380963/Evaluating_fair_trade_consumption _Politics_defetishization_and_producer_participation Accessed March 2016.

Mukherjee, Bharati. *Jasmine.* NY: Grove Press, 1989.

Pitman, John. "Double Consciousness". Stanford Encyclopedia of Philosophy. 2016. www.manasjournal.org/pdf_library/VolumeXXXI_1978/XXXI-20.pdf

Pradhan, Monica. *Hindi Bindi Club.* Bantam, 2007.

Ray, Raka. "Feminism and the History of the Indian Nation." *Contemporary Sociology*, vol. 33, no. 6, 2004, pp. 640–642.

"Social Construction of Reality Theory." www.encyclopedias5.com/encyclopedia-of-public-relations/3071-social-construction-of-reality-theory.html

Spivak, Gayatri c. "Can the Subaltern Speak." *Colonial Discourse and Post Colonial Theory*, Ed Patrick Williams and Laura Chrisman, 2009, pp. 129–186.

Spivak, Gayatri Chakravorty. "Situation Feminism." 26 Feb. 2010, Berkley, University of California, *Beatrice Bain Research*. www.youtube.com/watch?v=garPdV7U3fQ Accessed January 2017.

Spivak, Gayatri Chakravorty. "The Subaltern and the Popular: The Trajectory of the Subaltern in My Work". September 2004. Voices: A USCB Series. California, Berkley. *History of Art and Architecture and Film Studies*.

Sutherland, Sally. "Sita and Draupadi: Aggressive Behavior and Female Role Models in the Sanskrit Epics." *Journal of American Oriental Society.* JSTOR.

The Laws of Manu translated by George Buller. www.sacred-texts.com/hin/manu.htm

The Mahabharata translated by R.K. Narayan. Chicago Press, 2000.

The Ramayana translated by R. K. Narayan. Penguin, 1972.

Thapar, Romila. *The History of India*. Volume 1. Penguin, 1990.

Water. Movie. Dir. Deepa Mehta, 2005.

Teaching Literacy Through a Cultural Studies Approach to London
by John Pruitt

As the only literature instructor at my campus, I must meet the academic needs of a broad spectrum of readers who take my courses in order to meet the Humanities designation required for fulfilling the Associate of Arts and Science degree. Frankly, I want nothing more than to encourage reading beyond and outside of school and appreciating literature's ability to cultivate the imagination and call us to account as humans. Still, faced with a list of learning outcomes and a student body with varying abilities and expectations, I've experimented with the two extremes of literary study in order to cultivate a critical eye toward analyzing literary works for their structure and meaning: 1) basic close reading, such as tracing a symbol or image through a novel, which bores my advanced students, and 2) formal literary scholarship involving reading and incorporating into research papers sources drawn from the MLA International Bibliography, which alienates the less advanced.

Before enrolling in any literature course, students must earn at least a C in or exempt English 101 (College Writing and Critical Reading), the introductory degree-credit course covering the writing process from invention to editing, peer critique, revision, and reflection, a process applicable to writing assignments across disciplines. In this way, I view English 101 as a prerequisite not just to literature courses, but to most courses, for the threshold concepts and principles of rhetoric and composition covered here and in its successor, English 102 (Critical Writing, Reading, and Research), should transfer across disciplines for further cultivation. So, when I became a fellow with the Greater Madison (GMWP) site of the National Writing Project in 2015, I proposed a four-semester action research project focusing on the transfer of library skills from first-year composition into 200-level literature courses through a cultural studies approach to Literary London.

English 279: Women Writers (Fall 2015)
English 266: Modern Literature (Spring 2016)
English 267: Contemporary Literature (Fall 2016)
English 281: Special Topics—Horror and Speculative Fiction (Spring 2017)

Seeking to motivate students to transfer skills consciously across disciplines and situations, I sought to create meaningful research-based assignments and the pedagogy to further develop these skills incrementally through a program of course-integrated instruction.[1]

Prior Learning and the Challenges of Information Literacy

Because one core component of both English 101 and English 102 covers informal and rigorous research processes, from the short interview with a classmate to searches through library databases, I sought means of likewise integrating information literacy into the learning processes of my literature courses. In 2015, the Association of College and Research Libraries (ACRL) proposed a definition of information literacy as "the set of integrated abilities encompassing the reflective discovery of information, the understanding of how information is produced and valued, and the use of information in creating new knowledge and participating ethically in communities of learning." With this definition driving my project, I sought to discover how assignments shaped by the ACRL's information literacy threshold concepts affect depth of literary reading and encourage independent use of a variety of sources to increase comprehension, thus encouraging their continued use.

This emphasis on prior learning and concurrent knowledge, with an equal emphasis on metacognitive processes, requires that our students develop an awareness of themselves as learners, particularly when they understand the application and transfer of skills as relevant learning outcomes. Carrying the conversation beyond the

Frankly, I want nothing more than to encourage reading beyond and outside of school and appreciating literature's ability to cultivate the imagination and call us to account as humans.

FYC classroom, the contributors to Kathleen Johnson and Steven Harris's landmark collection *Teaching Literary Research* acknowledge the need for greater collaboration between literature instructors and librarians to develop this metacognition through assignments teaching research strategies within specific methodologies. As Van Hillard suggests in the opening chapter, students, instructors, and librarians alike must consider the library "not as some vast storehouse of data, but rather as an elaborate house of argument, a site where users activate and reactivate conversations and disagreements across time and space" (16). Furthermore, as our students increasingly consume technology while struggling with effective research methods, we must continue to help them understand when information is needed, where to find it, and how to evaluate and use it.

Along with the sheer growth of available information, the multiplicity of interfaces and media through which information becomes available encumbers its processing. In the programmatic document "Information Literacy Competency Standards for Higher Education," the ACRL points out that "increasingly, information comes to individuals in unfiltered formats, raising questions about its authenticity, validity, and reliability." Still, the Pew Research Center's recently published report *Information Overload* reveals that only 20% of American adults feel overwhelmed by the daily amount of information consumed. For those comfortable with this volume, nearly half oppose the ACRL's argument: despite the unfiltered format of delivery, 41% feel confident in their ability to evaluate this information.

However, a different story emerges when Americans interact with multiple institutions: according to 46% of those interviewed, the more institutions one interacts with regularly—institutions such as schools, banks, churches, and government offices—the more vexing it becomes to gather, track, and evaluate the information they provide. Thus, the report's author, John Horrigan, suggests that "information overload is situational: Specific situations may arise, such as when institutions impose high information demands on people for transactions, which create a sense of information burden" (4). Of course, academic research projects fall into these situations that often end in frustration and fatigue. As many instructors know, search engines such as Google dominate this delivery of unfiltered information to our students, thus inundating them as much as online academic databases do. For librarian Andrew Asher, "Google's design approaches have become standard expectations for all search tools, including those in the library. In particular, students expect features such as a single search box and relevancy-ranked search results as well as the ability to utilize natural language keyword search" (144). In other words, for many students, anything useful on the web, and thus for academic research projects, can be located on the first page of results uncovered through a Google search.

Because I require library orientations in all of my courses, for this project I surveyed my literature students—some of whom had already taken at least one of my FYC or literature courses—at the beginning of each semester in order to gauge their experience and comfort with conducting such research. From this survey, I learned that most had not attended a library orientation session within the past year (Table 1).

Based on this same survey, I also discovered that the majority had completed at least one assignment within the past year requiring in-text and/or bibliographic citations (Table 2).

Understanding their plight during the first semester of data collection (and consistently onward), I sought to design a series of assignments to meet this challenge through the integration of cultural studies based on three frameworks: the ACRL's information literacy threshold concepts, the WPA's "Framework," and Bloom's Taxonomy.[2]

Table 1: Students attending library orientation within the past year.

	ENG 279 Fall 2015	ENG 266 Spring 2016	ENG 267 Fall 2016	ENG 281 Spring 2017
Yes	4	13	4	10
No	13	14	14	15
Not enrolled	3	0	1	0
Total enrollment	**20**	**27**	**19**	**25**

Table 2: Number of assignments requiring documentation within the past year.

	ENG 279 Fall 2015	ENG 266 Spring 2016	ENG 267 Fall 2016	ENG 281 Spring 2017
10 or more	0	0	0	0
7–9	0	0	0	0
4–6	5	11	5	5
1–3	10	8	5	12
0	5	8	9	8
Total enrollment	**20**	**27**	**19**	**25**

Literary London and Cultural Studies

As preeminent critic Raymond Williams argues in his now classic *Culture and Society*, studying culture requires turning to a wide variety of discourses, "not only to the rich source of literature, but also to [. . .] the whole body of learning" (248), that is, to the interdisciplinary mechanisms of cultural production and consumption. Building on Williams' argument, Robert Scholes defines literary texts, like all texts, as social, historical, and political documents. Through textual studies, Scholes continues, "Our favorite works of literature need not be lost in this new enterprise, but the exclusivity of literature as a category must be discarded" (16). Because most of my students will major in fields other than English, it matters little to me that they read from the canon. Rather, I teach novels as imaginative pieces conditioned by the world in which their authors live(d), a world constructed of multiple competing texts that collaboratively articulate meaning.

With the study of London at the heart of this approach, I assign primary texts set in the city's central and suburban areas and that speak to how this setting contextualizes the plot and characters in relation to their points of reference and public spaces (see right).

In process, we cover the social, political, and economic movements while examining each text's relationship to commercial, popular, and high art standards, particularly in the context of how they better help us understand life in modern and contemporary London. The following assignments, activities, and student writing are representative examples drawn from teaching Lowndes' novel *The Lodger*, the first major text in the Horror and Speculative Fiction course.

English 279: Women Writers
Virginia Woolf, *Flush* (1933)
Muriel Spark, *Girls of Slender Means* (1963)
Maureen Duffy, *Capital* (1976)
Barbara Vine, *King Solomon's Carpet* (1991)
Zadie Smith, *White Teeth* (2000)

English 266: Modern Literature
Joseph Conrad, *The Secret Agent* (1903)
T. S. Eliot, *The Love Song of J Alfred Prufrock* (1915)
Virginia Woolf, *Mrs Dalloway* (1925)
George Orwell, *Keep the Aspidistra Flying* (1936)
Patrick Hamilton, *Hangover Square* (1941)

English 267: Contemporary Literature
Colin MacInnes, *Absolute Beginners* (1959)
Angela Carter, *The Magic Toyshop* (1967)
Doris Lessing, *The Good Terrorist* (1985)
Hanif Kureishi, *The Buddha of Suburbia* (1990)
Ian McEwan, *Saturday* (2005)

English 281: Special Topics—
Horror and Speculative Fiction
Marie Lowndes, *The Lodger* (1913)
Frank Baker, *The Birds* (1936)
Gerald Kersh, *Fowlers End* (1957)
J. G. Ballard, *High-Rise* (1975)
China Miéville, *King Rat* (1998)

Introducing the Course through QFT

Shannon Reed's and Kirilka Stavreva's approaches to teaching information literacy in literature courses sparked my initial interest, particularly Reed's assignment designed for a first-year writing course on censorship: She charged her students independently to identify a need for information from their assigned reading (e.g., about an unfamiliar word, idea, or location), consult the print resources in the library's reference section in order to appease that curiosity, and address in writing how that discovery enhanced an understanding of the reading assignment.

The prompt intrigued me, but my experience indicated that my students have difficulty independently identifying and articulating a need for information to elucidate literary texts. When I proposed this research project to GMWP, the site coordinators referred me to Dan Rothstein and Luz Santana's *Make Just One Change: Teach Students to Ask Their Own Questions* (2011), which introduces the Question Formulation Technique (QFT), designed to help students generate, improve, prioritize, and use questions by following this group process:

1. The instructor chooses a brief and simply stated phrase with a clear focus to inspirit questioning among the class (the Question Focus, or QFocus).
2. The instructor establishes rules for producing questions in groups.
3. Students produce questions.
4. Students improve questions by changing close-ended to open-ended and *vice versa*.
5. Students prioritize questions.[3]

Such a practice requires from students an intellectual flexibility, an epistemological shift from one who answers to one who asks. For example, during the first week, for the purpose of introducing the semester-long theme, I scaffolded the QFT with the QFocus phrase "horrors of everyday life" and allowed anyone to contribute questions that I in turn recorded on the whiteboard. Over ten minutes, we compiled this list:

1. What makes something horrible?
2. Can little things be horrible?
3. How do people handle horrible situations?
4. How dramatic does something have to be to be considered horrible?
5. What kind of horrors do rich people experience?
6. Is going without food a horror?
7. Is being unemployed a horror?
8. Can going to work be a horror?
9. How horrible is it to lose your phone?
10. How horrible is it to lose your phone if you're stranded or lost?
11. Is taking care of a sick relative a horror or a responsibility?
12. Is there a difference between a horror and a responsibility?
13. What can we do to end the horrors we live through every day?
14. Can we end these horrors if we're not rich and white?
15. Will there always be horrors in everyday life?
16. Is one horror just replaced by a different one?

I wasn't sure what to expect from this exercise as many unfamiliar students populated this class, but this QFocus provided a great deal of insight into them: as I conducted a Socratic seminar based on these questions, I found that this statement required introspection, the need for them to look into their own definitions, perspectives, interests, and histories. Just as the required novels for this course focused significantly on social class, my students, raised in this working-class community, did the same.

Making Sense of Novels through QFT

Lowndes' novel *The Lodger* fictionalizes the 1888 Jack the Ripper murders: briefly, Mr and Mrs Bunting rent a room in their home to a man they begin to suspect is The Avenger, a murderer of inebriated women in London's destitute East End. Because of this setting and the ubiquity of Jack the Ripper throughout popular culture, we completed a pre-reading QFT activity: I divided the class into five groups, each assigned to generate a list of questions over ten minutes based on the QFocus phrase "where we live influences the choices we make." Afterwards, each group followed the steps of QFT by *categorizing* their lists into open- and close-ended questions and discussing the advantages and disadvantages of each category. At this point, I revealed that the pending novel and contextual readings about the East End grapple with the strained correlation between cleanliness and morality. Based on that prompt, each group began *prioritizing* their questions, that is, choosing three that might focus their thinking on this theme. As each group finalized this short list, I wrote their questions on the whiteboard for them to justify. I also emphasized that these questions would lead to projects requiring library research. After debates and a silent vote via the Poll Everywhere app, they selected the following for us to investigate and discuss together while reading the primary sources:

1. Do we unconsciously judge messy people as liars, cheaters, and thieves, and neat people as more congenial?
2. If we move from a clean place to a dirty place or the other way around, how does our behavior change?
3. Why do people always comment on how clean or unkempt we look?

Jigsaw Readings: An Introduction to Primary Sources

Continuing with cooperative learning activities, once these three questions became the focus of *The Lodger*, I implemented a jigsaw activity to introduce contextual readings on the East End, primary sources detailing first-hand accounts of the extreme overcrowding and high concentration of both indigent and refugee immigrant populations. Based on Elliot Aronson's teaching strategy developed during the 1970s, the jigsaw technique breaks classes into groups and breaks assignments into separate parts that the groups assemble, thus requiring students to depend on each other to succeed.[4] I began by spending one class session explaining the significance of primary texts to literary and historical scholarship, as texts providing the raw evidence to analyze and interpret the past. I also modeled close reading and annotation, which cultivate habits of critical engagement with texts beyond underlining or highlights, through a Think-Aloud of chapter 24 of Jack London's *The People of the Abyss* (1903). In this ethnographic account, London contrasts newspapers that "boastfully proclaim that there is nothing the matter with the East End as a living place for men and women" with metaphorical descriptions of the area's inhabitants, "creatures of prey" and "twisted monstrosities" whose hands resemble "the paws of a gorilla." By projecting the chapter onto the SMARTBoard, I highlighted words, phrases, and sentences, and annotated with questions, comments, connections, patterns, themes, and observations specific to my reading of London's purpose and intended audience and to my own understanding of the East End. For example:

The dear soft people of golden theatres and wonder-mansions of the West End do not see these creatures, do not dream that they exist. But they are here, alive, very much alive in their jungle. And woe the day, when England is fighting in her last trench, and her able-bodied men are on the firing line! For on that day they will crawl out of their dens and lairs, and the people of the West End will see them, as the dear soft aristocrats of Feudal France saw them and asked one another, "Whence came they?" "Are they me?"	What separates the West End from the East End if none of these people see each other? Is there a barrier or understood boundaries? This is strange. Are the West End men keeping the East Enders away? Does this suggest that if there's a war, the East Enders will invade the West End because the fit men will be away fighting?

At the end of the session, I divided the class into five different groups, each with a common reading assignment:

1. Excerpts from John Milner Fothergill's *The Town Dweller: His Needs and His Wants* (1889)
2. Excerpts from George Augustus Sala's *Gaslight and Daylight with Some London Scenes They Shine Upon* (1859)
3. Excerpts from William Booth's *In Darkest England and the Way Out* (1890)
4. "Blind-Man's Buff" from *Punch* (22 September 1888)
5. "The Nemesis of Neglect" from *Punch* (29 September 1888)

For homework, I required each student to annotate the text independently through a close reading seeking out the central ideas and key supporting details providing insight into the East End such as gender roles; race relations; political or economic issues; work/career choices; leisure

activities; relationships; status; taste/style; aging; or foreign/international relations. During the next session, as I circulated to check the annotations, each group congregated to discuss its particular text and often continued to annotate as new revelations surfaced. During the following session, in true jigsaw form, at least one representative from each group met together in order to discuss the six documents together (including *People of the Abyss*) in order to assess their understanding of the East End and compile a list of questions stemming from their curiosity about this area. For these purposes, I suggested, like Reed, that the questions focus on a word, idea, allusion, reference, or location, in other words a research question asked simply for seeking out information. By referencing my annotations, I began with my own inquiry into the physical borders of the East End, if respectable women and children were warned never to cross particular streets or bridges or wander aimlessly after dark too close to particular neighborhoods. These questions, I said, would lead to the promised library research assignment.

At the end of this session, I assigned a one-minute paper asking them to reflect on the impact of marking directly on texts toward better understanding. Through this activity, I learned that "We couldn't write in our books in high school, so I never got in the habit," and that "I think writing right on the paper instead of the computer would help me more so I'm going to start printing these readings." My favorite response confessed that "We learned about this in 102, but I never did it because I just like to highlight, but I usually forget what I read as soon as I finish, so I'm going to start writing in all of my books to help me remember." While at the lowest levels of Bloom's Taxonomy, this ability to recall and comprehend basic information must still be honed through course-integrated instruction, particularly in our reluctant or developing readers.

Library Research: An Introduction to Reference Tools

When we met in the library the next day, with questions about the East End in hand, I introduced the class to the reference section and various reference databases, tools and genres more useful for purposes of quick information than for rigorous research, depending on the type of information sought. First, I reminded everyone of my own question specific to the boundaries of the East End and asked which type of information I was seeking:

1. *Definitions*, found in general or specialized dictionaries
2. *Background*, found in general or specialized encyclopedias or handbooks
3. *Statistical*, found in almanacs
4. *Geographical*, found in atlases or gazetteers

Once they determined that I sought geographical information, we considered the possible sources. Whereas some turned immediately to atlases, others suggested that an encyclopedia may prove as useful if the various maps of London failed to delineate the boundaries of the East End clearly. As one group discovered in Peter Barber's *London: A History in Maps*, which I'd pulled for this exercise, some artificial and geographical markers seem to enclose the area: the walls of the City of London to the west, the Thames to the south, and the Lea to the east. This group also showcased J. Reynolds' map of the East End (1882), which details a number of fields now lost to industrial and housing development, and Charles Booth's map (1889) comprehensively describing the spatial distribution of poverty throughout the city.

From this brief lesson, I charged the class to keep, edit, or write new questions if inspired by the economic and agricultural information provided by these maps; to determine the type

of information they sought; and to find reference sources that might help them appease that curiosity. By the end of the session, I found many students working collaboratively. For example, a group of nursing students sought background information on diseases prevalent in the East End from Bynum and Porter's *Companion Encyclopedia of the History of Medicine* and from Kiple's *The Cambridge World History of Human Disease*. A different group expressed interest in seeking background information on services to assist the poor in the East End. When reference materials such as Davies' *Blackwell Encyclopedia of Social Work* produced no results, they reconsidered the subject terms and turned instead to the history of economics, which resulted in discoveries about the evolution of the Poor Laws through the nineteenth century from Mokyr's *The Oxford Encyclopedia of Economic History*. Ultimately, through informal feedback, I learned that such inquiry-based tasks, from writing questions to finding answers based on one's own interests, reminded everyone of the importance of annotating and actively seeking out areas of interest that may become the subject of research projects.

By the end of the session, I found many students working collaboratively.

As we read and annotated the novel itself, I presented two additional challenges. By repeatedly reviewing the QFT questions on cleanliness and morality, we analyzed textual evidence describing Mrs Bunting as a detective with the ability to observe her lodger's behavior covertly because of her domestic responsibilities and expectations (e.g., cleaning his room, delivering meals), thus gendering her knowledge as inherently feminine. We also discussed the role of newspapers and their effects on the morality of readers who identify with a murderer who purges the streets of depraved women, all in a political climate often warning women and children to avoid impure literature. As we finished, I presented the first challenge: to find and annotate through close reading a primary source contributing to our understanding of *The Lodger* and the

link between cleanliness and morality during the late-nineteenth and early-twentieth century. In order to direct them, I showcased a number of archives and libraries such as the British Library, the National Archives, and Cambridge Digital Library websites, plus open databases such as *The Reading Experience Database, 1450-1945*, and *EuroDocs: History of the United Kingdom*. By allotting time to maneuvering through and acclimating to these sites, I watched the students help each other through the process by experimenting with search terms and finding distraction in photos that piqued their curiosity.

When the class submitted their annotations, I presented a second challenge: to conduct a database or library catalog search for three scholarly secondary sources that, based only on their abstracts, may clarify the information presented by the primary source. I focused not on comprehending the often esoteric writing in academic journal articles targeting audiences well beyond our first- and second-year students. Instead, the class practiced search strategies and experimented with search terms by completing a research narrative, a log of the steps taken and thought processes that contributed to discovering more about a topic in order to conceptualize an effective research strategy. To this end, I targeted two elements defining the information literate according to the ACRL's competency standards: those who can "assess the needed information effectively and efficiently" and "evaluate information and its sources critically." I anticipated that this active learning component to studying *The Lodger* would communicate the integral nature of information literacy to course content.

During the introduction to library databases, the senior academic librarian based his lesson on a question inspired by Jack London's observation in *People of the Abyss* of "brass-buttoned keepers" who maintained order when the East End's atavistic denizens "snarled too fiercely": what guidelines were London's police force required to follow while maintaining order? Because such a question spoke to the inundation of current news reports of police shootings of unarmed citizens in St.

Paul, Milwaukee, and other cities, I thought my students would appreciate the topical connection. By intentionally walking through the process as if for the first time, the librarian discussed search vocabulary, Boolean operators, and subject databases while reinforcing three important truths: research can be frustrating, tedious, and rewarding, all regardless of level of experience. By the end, we'd discovered book chapters and articles on the histories of the Metropolitan Police Service and the City of London Police, each organization dating to the early nineteenth century.

When the students began their own searches, I required them to write and reflect through a narrative detailing the research process:

1. the process of narrowing or broadening the research topic based on initial search attempts
2. the process of locating and choosing the appropriate library research databases or search tools based on their usefulness and difficulty
3. the awareness of a successful or unsuccessful search strategy based on search terms, keywords, and subjects headings and tags
4. a reflection on the research process in general

For example, one student, JD, discovered Hallie Killick's *The Ideal Home and Its Problems* (1911), a treatise on domesticity prefaced by "Rules for Our Household," written by her husband, Olympic tennis champion Sir Eustace Miles, shortly after their marriage. In this section's annotation, JD drew attention to the role of servants, the subject of his investigation:

But neither the man nor the woman should do for the servants what the servants are paid to do for the master and mistress. The mistress should be able to perform every single detail of household work herself. But if she is constantly depriving the servants of their duties (which are part of their daily moral food) she is a bad mistress. The successful managers are those who can do the work for themselves, but delegate it to others whom they supervise. The servants need not be bullied and sweated. They need not be spoken to rudely and angrily. For the authority of managers ultimately depends not on terrorism but on justice.	In this paragraph it looks like he's saying that servants feed themselves it looks like religiously through their work because he calls it their "daily moral food" like "give us this day our daily bread." I have a hard time believing this because Eustace is upper class so he wouldn't do the housework if there weren't servants but it looks like he'd be a good boss because he wants to make sure at least to the readers that he cares about the servants' souls. This makes me wonder what servants thought their responsibilities were and if they also connected work with moral responsibility and a clean house.

In his research narrative, JD immediately turned to his initial, fruitless search:

I used the History Reference Center, Humanities International Complete, Literary Reference Center, and MLA International Bibliography. When I searched for "servants" and "morals" I only got 22 hits (yay!), but they were mostly old books in Masterplots. Since all those books are in Literary Reference Center I took off that database. That left 4, but the abstracts weren't about the right things.

But something interesting happened when JD manipulated the search terms "servants," "London," and "morals." As subject terms used together, they delivered zero results. However, "when I made them all just keywords, I got 7 hits. That shows it's important to know what to put in the drop

down list. I still didn't get anything I can use though." Irritation with the assignment intensified when he expanded his search to all databases available in Academic Search Complete: "I got 18 hits with keywords 'servants,' 'morals,' and 'nineteenth century' but nothing I can use! How hard can it be to find information about servants?" Finally, two possible sources materialized:

> I found a chapter from a book called Social Control in Europe 1800-2000 called "Caring or controlling? The East End of London in the 1880s and 1890s" by Rosemary O'Day. The abstract says it's about the middle class helping instead of controlling the poor, so even though it's not about servants, there are similarities because of class. I found it because I changed "nineteenth century" to "Victorian" in the library catalog, also giving me a book called Life below stairs: domestic servants in England from Victorian times by Frank E. Huggett. This was frustrating but it showed me again that the right search words are important.

When reflecting on how these sources together—*The Ideal Home* and the secondary sources— helped him better understand *The Lodger*, he revealed that "Having context to support the literature being read, it's easier to understand just where the author is coming from and even why they're writing it in the first place." Specific to Lowndes' novel, he wrote that "with the Buntings as the home owners, even the most questionable people can rent a room and stay for a while as tenants." Crucial to this reflection, and without my prompting, JD activated his prior knowledge based in his own social class as the students did during the initial QFocus on "the horrors of everyday life": "This context is relevant because the Buntings used to be servants, which was not uncommon or undignified. It is now, though, because my mom has been cleaning houses my whole life, and

she's not treated or paid well for what that's done to her body." His focus turns to articulating his knowledge within the social context of his family and within the institutional context of the classroom: "I don't know if this is art imitating life or life imitating art, but I've learned through my life and from reading these things that servants aren't seen the same any more." Both literary and historical context enabled JD to articulate and affirm his experiential knowledge as valid within the context of the classroom. In other words, through reflection on this particular research-based assignment, he focused on acquiring new knowledge by discovering the changing perception of servants over a century.

The Transfer of Research Skills Across the Disciplines

At the end of the semester, I asked the class to write statements reflecting on the process of conducting research, on what they believed had transferred from their FYC course(s) to use in this new writing and research context, and the knowledge they'd acquired about this process in ENG 281 to transfer to across disciplines. This excerpt came from the opening to the first statement I read:

> This semester gave way to a lot of annoying research, leading me into frustrating databases and deplorable situations where I had to struggle to find exactly what I wanted. Most of the sources I would have already had to know about if I wanted to use them, so perhaps I just was able to use the databases provided in a coherent manner? Perhaps I'm just a dimwit that cannot understand how to handle a computer? I'm more inclined to agree with my rhetorical questions more so than refuting them. Sometimes I see myself more of a buffoon than an intelligent college student.

Based on this response, I may have failed a bit: although it's unstated, I wondered if this student carried a preconceived idea of what the ideal primary and secondary source looked like as "I had to struggle to find exactly what I wanted." Perhaps many of us do. As stated by another, "The process of finding the perfect source is part of the learning. If primary sources were easy to find, then this probably wouldn't even be an assignment." The diction interests me because I hear it in my FYC courses as well, the quest for the "perfect source." This student continues with an intriguing observation: "it seems as though you can find anything BUT what you're looking for. You may even come across a source that you like more than what you were originally looking for. So, this has been a fun learning assignment."

Plugged in or not, they must still leave the academy with the information literacy skills that will serve them in and out of a variety of research and writing situations.

But what are they looking for through the research process?

My priority, as stated, was to insure that my students developed and enhanced their existing transferable relationship with the library and that they would apply critical thinking techniques while conducting library research across disciplines. My interest lay less in a mastery of the mechanics of a particular database, but rather in the ability to make discerning choices about the information found. One of the nursing students mentioned above wrote that, "I'm glad I learned about the history of diseases in London a hundred years ago because I can see how they were diagnosed and think about that in my nursing classes." Most, however, focused on their first exposure to library resources. As one exasperated student explained, "My history teacher made us do research in the library but no one showed me how, which was so unfair and I got a bad grade. The research is hard to do but I feel a little better about it now because I know other teachers will want that." She's right.

Although it pains me that students rarely enter the library to conduct research, I believe that the stationary and portable electronic devices disseminated across campuses enable their users more independently to set their own research goals and assume increasing responsibility for planning and enacting their own learning activities. Plugged in or not, they must still leave the academy with the information literacy skills that will serve them in and out of a variety of research and writing situations. Furthermore, while many factors contribute to the degree of mental effort they expend on their assignments, the value they perceive in these tasks ranks among them. The metacognitive writing—the one-minute papers and especially the research narrative requiring reflection on their thinking and learning—exposed such value by making them aware of the necessity of transferring or adapting their learning to new contexts and tasks. They also became aware of their strengths and weaknesses as learners and researchers by acknowledging the limits of their knowledge and then considering how to expand that knowledge. Once they accept the truths stated by my senior academic librarian, that research can be frustrating, tedious, and rewarding, I hope that they'll continue to develop their information literacy skills during the futile search for that "perfect source."

End Notes

1. All references to students are anonymous or pseudonymous. I collected the included excerpts of student writing with IRB approval and was guided by the CCCC Guidelines for Conduct of Ethical Research in Composition Studies.
2. Logistically, I face one additional obstacle: at my small campus of 900 students, neither of the two librarians holds a full-time position, thus hindering both collaboration and assistance during evening hours and weekends. Although I always present them with my syllabus and assignment guidelines, quite often they must cede bibliographic instruction to me because of their availability.
3. Refer to the book's website at http://rightquestion.org/make-just-one-change/ for additional information plus blog posts and discussion boards.
4. Refer to Aronson's website *Jigsaw Classroom* at https://www.jigsaw.org for resources on facilitating these activities at multiple grade levels.

Works Cited

Asher, Andrew D. "Search Epistemology: Teaching Students about Information Discovery." *Not Just Where to Click: Teaching Students How to Think about Information*, edited by Troy A. Swanson and Heather Jagman, ACRL, 2015, pp. 139-54.

Association of College and Research Libraries. "Framework for Information Literacy for Higher Education." *American Library Association*, 11 Jan. 2016, www.ala.org/acrl/standards/ilframework. Accessed 18 May 2017.

Council of Writing Program Administrators, et al. *Framework for Success in Postsecondary Writing*. Jan. 2011, wpacouncil.org/files/framework-for-success-postsecondary-writing.pdf. Accessed 30 June 2017.

Hillard, Van E. "Information Literacy as Situated Literacy." *Teaching Literary Research: Challenges in a Changing Environment*, edited by Kathleen A. Johnson and Steven R. Harris, ACRL, 2009, pp. 11-21.

Horrigan, John B. *Information Overload*. 7 Dec. 2016. *Pew Research Center*, www.pewinternet. org/2016/12/07/information-overload/.

"Information Literacy Competency Standards for Higher Education." *Association of College and Research Libraries*, 2000, www.ala.org/acrl/standards/informationliteracycompetency. Accessed 18 May 2017.

Reed, Shannon L., and Kirilka Stavreva. "Layering Knowledge: Information Literacy as Critical Thinking in the Literature Classroom." *Pedagogy*, vol. 6, no. 3, 2006, pp. 435-52. *Education Research Complete*, doi:10.1215/15314200-2006-004.

Rothstein, Dan, and Luz Santana. *Make Just One Change: Teach Students to Ask Their Own Questions*. 5th ed., Harvard Education, 2014.

Scholes, Robert. *Textual Power: Literary Theory and the Teaching of English*. Yale UP, 1985.

Williams, Raymond. *Culture and Society, 1780-1950*. Columbia UP, 1958.

Literary Cures for Common-Sense Thinking in the Composition Classroom

by Andrew Bishop

For almost two years now, I have been teaching one of my favorite courses at Hudson County Community College (HCCC) in Jersey City: the English 102 Literature Variation. It is a college-level composition course focused on argument and research, but a variation designed, supposedly, for students who have a passion for literature. I say "supposedly" only because, when students enroll in the course, they do not always notice the "LIT" subject code we put by the course title to signify "Literature Variation." So generally the class looks something like this: a number of students who are there by accident or for scheduling reasons; a handful of others who enjoy reading literature but are not pursuing a Liberal Arts English Option, the closest thing we offer at HCCC to an English major; and then perhaps the one or two students who have, indeed, enrolled in community college to study literature.

Naturally, this situation raises some questions: why am I having composition students read short stories, poems, and plays when they may never again, in any course they take in college, have to analyze similar material? Why at HCCC do we offer a Literature Variation of Composition II when the college has no English major, only an English "option" for students whose official major is still Liberal Arts? And more generally, why integrate literature into composition?

This last question about the role of literature in composition is one which people have been debating for over twenty years. So before I give my own response, I should give some context: as essay titles like Erika Lindemann's "Freshman Composition: No Place for Literature," and more recently, Gregory Schafer's "The Problem of Literature in Composition Classes" suggest, many scholars are opposed to the inclusion of literature in composition courses. They fear that literature generates too much "teacher talk," too little authentic dialogue (Lindemann 312); they fear that literature leads to a text-centered class which neglects the writing and research process rather than a student-centered class which explores the writing and research process (313); they fear that great Literature, with a capital L, has too much of an aura attached to it, an aura which inspires "reverence and veneration" rather than inquiry, distance and passivity rather than "rebellious energy" (Schafer 35, 37); and they fear that essays on "the ingrown toenail motif in *Beowulf*" will not prepare students for writing in other disciplines (Lindemann 314).

These are legitimate fears. And with Lindemann and Schafer, I agree: the composition course should not, under any circumstances, become a course in literary appreciation. But the fact is most *literature* courses today are not courses solely in literary appreciation; they are opportunities, as Emily Isaacs puts it, to embrace "the study of literature for social, cultural, and political inquiry" (110).[1] Moreover, they are not necessarily taught by professors more interested in the minutia of majestic language than students. When we misrepresent these courses as primarily about transformative encounters with "magical or transcendent" texts, great works which are "miraculously good," (Elbow 535), we, like Peter Elbow, assume far more "disciplinary difference" than actually exists between the fields of literary studies and composition (Isaacs 108). In 2002, Peter Elbow wrote, "The Cultures of Literature and Composition: What Could Each Learn from the Other?" an opinion piece which, as Elbow himself admits, relies on some "large arguable generalizations" (534). Part of Elbow's goal was, admirably, to bridge the divide between these two "cultures" by reminding compositionists of the value and usefulness of "imaginative language" (537); however, he tends to represent literary scholars as professors who care more about imagery and metaphors than their students (536). After Elbow's essay was published, his colleague, Michael Mattison,

promptly challenged many of Elbow's conclusions: in "A Comment on 'The Cultures of Literature and Composition: What Could Each Learn from the Other?'" Mattison draws upon interviews with graduate teaching assistants to demonstrate the extent to which "a concern with students and their ideas is a part of literary studies" and descriptions of a wide "gulf" between the worlds of literature and composition are mistaken (441).

If it is wrong to assume that literature courses are necessarily teacher- and text-centered, it is certainly wrong to assume that assigning literature in a composition course

> *. . . why am I having composition students read short stories, poems, and plays when they may never again, in any course they take in college, have to analyze similar material?*

necessarily leads to a teacher- or text-centered class. In fact, like Michael Gamer, I do not see how assigning literature necessarily leads to anything. In "Fictionalizing the Disciplines: Literature and the Boundaries of Knowledge," Gamer writes, "Individual texts and disciplines do not determine pedagogy nearly so much as the choices of particular teachers in particular classrooms" (281). Fiction, in other words, can detract from or enhance a composition course; the issue is not so much the reading we assign but instead how we encourage our students to approach that reading and, ultimately, what we ask them to do with it.

In my English 102 Literature Variation, literature has several functions. At the risk of sounding too idealistic, I use literature, first and foremost, as a remedy for that stultifying sickness which inevitably infects us all: "common sense." In college, I had an intimidating Spanish literature professor who angrily forbid us from ever justifying an answer we provided with the phrase, "It's just common sense." He

despised "common sense" and felt it had no place in a literature class. At the time I didn't understand—now I do, so much so that I would say "common sense" also has no place in a composition course. Why? The art critic John Berger begins his influential book, *Ways of Seeing*, with the observation that "Seeing comes before words" (7), and I think it is precisely this kind of original seeing which our composition students need to engage in—the seeing which happens *before* "common sense" takes over and allows them to ostensibly "know" and categorize what they are seeing.

If we hope to clean our eyeglasses a bit, or to try on a new pair of lenses altogether, I cannot think of a better way than reading literature, because literature, more so than other forms of writing, puts us in minds and places where we have to look at our world as if "for the first time" (Shklovsky 779). This, at least, is what the Russian theorist, Viktor Shklovsky, claimed when he spoke of "defamiliarization," the way

art returns us to a moment when we knew less, or had fewer assumptions and habits, and therefore saw more (781). Literature explicitly deals with perception, "imparting," as Shklovsky notes, "the sensation of things as they are perceived and not as they are known" (778). Fiction offers us perspectives from which what we assume to be natural appears, through the eyes of a narrator, thoroughly unnatural. The first page of William Faulkner's novel, *As I Lay Dying*, gives us golf as it looks to Benjy, who is autistic and does not know what golf is. Ursula Le Guin's science-fiction novel, *The Dispossessed*, investigates capitalism from the perspective of Shevek, an anarchist physicist who has no conception of private property. Alternatively, literature also offers us perspectives from which what we assume to be unnatural appears, through the eyes of a narrator, thoroughly natural. William Blake's poem, "The Chimney Sweeper," from *Songs of Innocence*, depicts the brutal exploitation

of children from the perspective of a child chimney sweep who does not know he is being exploited; he views cleaning chimneys as his rightful "duty" (Blake 24). Charlotte Perkins Gillman's short story, "The Yellow Wallpaper," depicts emotional and marital neglect from the perspective of a mentally ill wife who does not know she is being neglected; as she states, "one expects this in marriage" (Gillman 317). "Ideology" is one word for this. But in all cases, what one literary text can do—again, if used correctly—is force our composition students to question the beliefs which blind people, the beliefs which can make anything and everything—golf, capitalism, child slavery, marriage, whatever—into completely "natural," God-given phenomena, rather than puzzling objects of inquiry.

By making the familiar and the habitual unfamiliar and unsettling, literature serves as a springboard for inquiry—another key role which fiction plays in my composition course.

I do not just mean inquiry into, to quote Erika Lindemann again, "the ingrown toenail motif in *Beowulf*." The many schools of critical theory—Marxist, feminist, psychoanalytic, historicist, eco-critical, queer, and so on—attest to the fact that literature can help us inquire about essentially anything *if* we approach literary texts as "cultural artifacts" (Isaacs 110). The "if" is important because, as Gregory Shafer notes, many of us still "read great works" with a "tacit sense of reverence and veneration . . . . Students who are invited to base their writing on literature tend to pay homage to the writer rather than making the work a springboard for their personal views" (35). Shafer's claim rings true to me: although my students may not have heard of, say, William Blake, they often approach his poems as one would a sacred text rather than a cultural artifact: they mine it for answers, not questions. But does this tendency amongst students mean that composition professors should abandon literature all together, as Schafer implies? Why not simply teach our students to approach literature in a different way, since, I would argue, there is nothing inherent in literary works that demands we revere them?

This is what I do by having students engage in Quescussion, an activity originally developed for teaching poetry by the English professor Paul Bidwell and discussed by Allan Gedalof in his book, *Teaching Poetry*. The activity not only divests students of their fears about literature but also, as Gedalof claims, inspires them to "take a measure of control over and responsibility for the nature and direction of their learning" (36). The idea is simple: as the funny and hard to pronounce name implies, Quescussion is "a form of discussion conducted through questions" (35). Students are presented with a statement, a poem, a video, an issue—in short, any brief text the instructor wants them to think deeply about—and then prohibited from making statements: rather than make statements, they must make questions. As the instructor, your role is simple: do not speak (unless you absolutely have to) and then record all the questions the students ask on the board, organizing them as you see fit.

I like this activity, in part, because there is something in it for all composition students, not just the future literary critic. Say I elect to play the game with William Blake's poem, "Nurse's Song," from *Songs of Experience*, one of my favorites because many of my students at HCCC are also young mothers:

> When the voices of children are heard on the green,
>   And whisperings are in the dale,
> The days of my youth rise fresh in my mind,
>   My face turns green and pale.
>
> Then come home, my children, the sun is gone down,
>   And the dews of night arise;
> Your spring and your day are wasted in play,
>   And your winter and night in disguise.

I can imagine, after some practice, the psychology major wondering, why do memories of her "youth" cause the nurse's "face" to turn "green and pale" (3-4)? Did something happen to her as a child? While the early-childhood education major is more interested in how or why the children are told not to play: is play not a crucial part of childhood development? Why does the nurse associate play with waste

Although it is fun to try, a good game of Quescussion is impossible to recreate.

(7)? Which then leads the history major, aware that this poem was published at the beginning of the Industrial Revolution in England, to ask: might the Industrial Revolution help explain this nurse's disdain for play? While the environmental studies major—who has, along with the entire class, also read Blake's other version of "Nurse's Song," from *Songs of Innocence*—wants to know: why are these children not outside on the vast and beautiful green depicted in the other poem? Why did Blake change the setting? And so on, as the relentless investigation continues.

Although it is fun to try, a good game of Quescussion is impossible to recreate. And, perhaps, noting the students' majors as I did is not an ideal way to represent what happens. Rather than commit to a specific discipline, literature can inspire composition students, as Gamer argues, to think "across the disciplines"—even see the disciplines as "human constructs that change constantly and even arbitrarily" (285–286). When playing Quescussion, students inevitably draw upon their predefined academic interests, those majors which they have, in some cases, been forced to declare. Nevertheless, when the activity

has ended, and my students and I, in a state of confusion or awe, gaze at the messy board where I have recorded the endless list of questions, students also are inevitably forced to think *beyond* their individual majors. In the game I just described, for example, that messy list of questions would tell students, amongst other things, that child-rearing is a thoroughly interdisciplinary issue, the complicated product of individual psychology, cultural and philosophical assumptions about work and play, economic history, and, also, the environments people have access to (as well as the health of those environments.)

After the list of questions is complete, the instructor can jump straight into discussion; however, another option is to give students snippets of relevant information from one discipline or another—a photograph of a child chimney sweep, a discussion of psychoanalytic ideas about repression and defense mechanisms, or maybe a Marxist discussion of alienation or exploitation—then ask: which of your questions can these sources or ideas help you to answer? The outside sources and concepts will keep the interdisciplinary engines running. It is like giving the students a tool bag and saying: which of these tools can you use? Or at least: which of these tools do you want to learn more about? Significantly, in this case, since students themselves have identified the problems, they will likely have more intrinsic motivation to take up the tools (the text, the theories, the history, each other) and work out a solution.

During each round of Quescussion, I always have my students record the questions they ask. This way, later, as I introduce students to critical theory, they can identify the lines of inquiry to which they are, for one reason or another, instinctually drawn. Students see to what extent their inquiries are similar to the questions typically asked by feminists, ecocritics, Marxists, psychoanalysts, or others.[2] Last semester I had a Hispanic radiology major, juggling school with being a single mother, who saw Marxist alienation in just about everything we read, while an aspiring African-American business student realized that she was—and perhaps had long been—a feminist. Now, let me explain: my goal is not to convert students to one ideology or another or to convert composition into critical theory. But I do like how, through "quescussing" a few literary texts and a bit of critical theory, my composition students developed commitments—new ways of seeing—which they can take into their respective majors but which also *transcend* any narrowly defined academic field of study: we have feminist novelists and businesswomen, Marxist historians and sociologists, and environmental philosophers and scientists. Part of me asks, "What does a radiology major need critical theory for?" Yet another part of me recognizes that this question does a horrible disservice to the student, the student who is a person, and not just a major.

. . . by asking students to engage with imaginative texts, and test out some different theoretical approaches, we can encourage our students to discover perspectives which may influence more than just their academic lives.

The late compositionist, Gary Tate, makes this point in his essay, "A Place for Literature in Composition;" while acknowledging that composition is, in part, about preparing students for writing in the disciplines, he reminds us that we also should prepare students for "writing beyond the disciplines," for the decisions they will make "*outside of the academy,* as they struggle to figure out how to live their lives—that is, how to vote and love and survive, how to respond to change and diversity and death and oppression and freedom" (320, his emphasis).

So when asked, "why integrate literature into composition?" my response is threefold. First, because with literature we can "de-familiarize" a wide range of phenomena, turning anything and everything into an engaging object of inquiry. Second, because with activities like Quescussion, we can teach students important interdisciplinary-thinking and problem-solving skills. And third, because by asking students to engage with imaginative texts, and test out some different theoretical approaches, we can encourage our students to discover perspectives which may influence more than just their academic lives. Surely, there are ways of doing each of these three things which do not involve literature. But literature is one form of composition. And considering that, as Emily Isaacs reminds us, many, if not most, composition instructors today have a background in literary studies (101), I see no reason to take literature off the table altogether.

End Notes

1. With the increasing significance of ecocriticism, we need to add "environmental inquiry" to Isaacs' list.
2. The Purdue OWL contains useful lists of "typical questions" associated with different schools of criticism. See their page on "Literary Theory."

Works Cited

Berger, John. *Ways of Seeing*. New York, 1973.

Blake, Williams. "The Chimney Sweeper." *Songs of Innocence and Experience*. e-book, Project Gutenberg, 2008.

    "Nurse's Song." *Songs of Innocence and Experience*. e-book, Project Gutenberg, 2008.

Elbow, Peter. "OPINION: The Cultures of Literature and Composition: What Could Each Learn from the Other?" *College English*, vol. 64, no. 5, 2002, pp. 533-546.

Gamer, Michael. "Fictionalizing the Disciplines: Literature and the Boundaries of Knowledge." *College English*, vol. 57, no. 3, 1995, pp. 281-286.

Gedalof, Allan J. *Teaching Poetry: A Handbook of Exercises for Large and Small Classes*. Norton, 2005.

Gilman, Charlotte Perkins. "The Yellow Wallpaper." *The Norton Introduction to Literature*. Portable 12th ed. Edited by Kelly J. Mays, New York, 2017, pp. 316-330

Isaacs, Emily. "Teaching General Education Writing: Is There a Place for Literature?" *Pedagogy*, vol. 9, no. 1, 2009, pp. 97-120.

Lindemann, Erika. "Freshman Composition: No Place for Literature." *College English*, vol. 55, no. 3, 1993, pp. 311-316.

"Literary Theory." *The Purdue OWL*. The Writing Lab and OWL at Purdue and Purdue U, 2008, owl.english.purdue.edu/owl. Accessed 25 Jan. 2018.

Mattison, Michael. "A Comment on 'The Cultures of Literature and Composition: What Could Each Learns from the Other?" *College English*, vol. 65, no. 4, 2003, pp. 439-441.

Schafer, Gregory. "The Problem of Literature in Composition Classes." *Language Arts Journal of Michigan*, vol. 28, no. 2, 2013, pp. 34-40.

Shklovsky, Viktor. "Art as Technique." *The Critical Tradition: Classic Texts and Contemporary Trends*. Third ed. Ed. David H. Richter. Boston: Bedford/St. Martin's, 2006. 774-785.

Tate, Gary. "A Place for Literature in Freshman Composition." *College English*, vol. 55, no. 3, 1993, pp. 317-321.

All Means All
by Lex Runciman

As 2017 has concluded and now a new year begun, a certain amount of distancing has been necessary for many of us. At least that has been the case for me. I have needed to figure out an internal way to blunt the worst of the current White House statements and actions, to at once resist but not be all-possessed by circumstance that, as one person, I have little immediate power to alter. Recent directly racist comments from the President have gotten through those defenses. As someone who spent an entire teaching career in the company of great American authors, I have, one way or another, often felt myself pointing to and emphasizing what I have understood as an American ideal, an American aspiration: to acknowledge and act and understand what it might mean to be a free person, with empathy for others as part of a shared, implicit and explicit agreement about what has been called "life, liberty, and the pursuit of happiness"—with the full understanding that we are all endowed at birth with "certain inalienable rights."

To illustrate, let me briefly discuss four texts that have been important to me over 35 years of teaching undergraduates. Though any number of novels suggest themselves, I'm thinking now of Zora Neale Hurston's *Their Eyes Were Watching God,* Tom Kromer's *Waiting for Nothing,* James Weldon Johnson's *Autobiography of an Ex-Coloured Man,* and Molly Gloss' *The Jump-Off Creek.*

In many ways, these four American works could not be more distinctly different, yet each revolves around a central character struggling to articulate an authentic voice, struggling to make at once an identity and a personal freedom each feels entitled to. In Hurston's novel, that character is Janie Crawford, returning to her hometown, Eatonville, "a town [made] all outa colored folks," after time away. Where's she been? What's she been doing? In her words, "Ah been a delegate to de big 'ssociation of life. Yessuh! De Grand Lodge, de big convention of livin' is just where Ah been dis year and a half y'all ain't seen me." Hurston's narrator, who knows Janie well, tells us, "Janie saw her life like a great tree in leaf with the things suffered, things enjoyed, things done and undone. Dawn and doom was in the branches."

I've always thought of this novel as double voiced. Janie tells much of her story herself, with that narrator often enough providing an overview. The two voices combine to make a testament, a witnessing, a voicing of American life rare in 1937 when this book was first published.

Published 25 years earlier, James Weldon Johnson's *Autobiography of an Ex-Coloured Man* is constructed to in all ways resemble autobiography. It is told in first person by an "ex-coloured man," a narrator light-skinned enough to pass as white, though to do so means living at once a white life and also a life of shame. He writes in order to disclose "the great secret of my life, the secret which for some years I have guarded far more carefully than any of my earthly possessions; and it is a curious study to me to analyze the motives which prompt me to do it."

That is, this narrator writes in order to tell his personal truth: to set the record straight, to acknowledge and affirm the wholeness of his identity, without deceit and without apology. Johnson creates a marvelous character. By turns a jazz pianist, a cigar roller, a gambler, and a real estate developer, European traveler and speaker of four languages, this character's life gives us a unique perspective from which to understand something of American experience of prejudice and segregation during that time between the Civil War and World War I. It's also a persuasive example of one character's effort to assert his right to be who he is, navigating his way despite social prejudice, all the while passing for white, and, in the end, ashamed that he could not or did not join "that small but gallant band of coloured men" who were "making history and a race," people who "have the eternal principles of right on their side."

Tom Kromer's novel also purports to be "strictly autobiographical," though, as the autobiographical note indicates, some events in it are portrayed out of their lived sequence "in order to better develop the story." Published in 1935 and carrying the dedication, "To Jolene,

who turned off the gas," *Waiting for Nothing* offers a first person account of a man "on the fritz," that is, "a stiff," that is, a person who in the deep shadows of The Depression lives by begging: "Most of the time I slept and ate in missions, dinged the streets and houses, and used every other racket known to stiffs to get by."

He is, in the idiom of the day, "a bum," and at every point, the telling in *Waiting for Nothing* dramatizes the distances between people "in the dough" and people hungry and on the streets: "I pass a joint. A ritzy place. It is all white inside. The tables are full. They are eating, and I am hungry. These guys pay good dough for a feed, and they are not even hungry." Later, having stolen a "gat" (a gun), he thinks seriously about robbing a bank: "What have I got to lose? Nothing. What have I got to live for? Soup and stale bread, that is what I have to live for. That is what I have to lose."

> *That is, this narrator writes in order to tell his personal truth: to set the record straight, to acknowledge and affirm the wholeness of his identity, without deceit and without apology.*

And then we have Lydia Sanderson, diarist and widow from Williamsport, Pennsylvania, a single woman living in the last decade of the 19th century and determined to make a new life for herself in the sparsely populated northeast corner of Oregon, where she has bought a homesteading claim sight unseen. Riding a mule, leading another as well as two goats, she arrives at last only to find that her new home is little more than a shack, "built with unskinned pine logs chinked poorly with mud and fern and moss . . . eight feet by twelve, no more than that, listing slightly to the south."

Her relevant diary entry reads this way: "Lost the way on poor directions but I am here now and glad for it, tho it is bad as I knew it would be, the stove rusted clear through, the

Zora Neale Hurston's book, Their Eyes Were Watching God.

roof rotted, the logs poor fitted and mildewed, the yard where the Animals must stand all Mud and stones . . . . There is a window, small & unglassed, but I believe it stands to let in the low Winter Sun from the South. I am greatly sore & tired, having come all day across these dark Mountains in unending rain." Molly Gloss' novel, *The Jump-Off Creek,* is Lydia's story as she works to make a subsistence and a new life for herself, turning down two proposals of marriage even as she makes an independence for herself among her far-flung neighbors.

For me, teaching these novels and others like them has meant engaging other readers in the complexities of characters' lives, thinking of them as actual persons that fiction and autobiography have given us access to in ways unavailable otherwise: in such characters we readers get to track the human complexities of motivation, thought, feeling, and action. And in the process of this reading and back-and-forth engagement, the class discussions thus provoked have often and inevitably noted the ways that such American novels are, at their core, aspirational. Each of the characters acts

from a set of foundational assumptions, and they are the assumptions of The Declaration of Independence: "We hold these truths to be self-evident, that all men are created equal, that they are endowed by their Creator with certain inalienable Rights, that among these are Life, Liberty and the pursuit of Happiness."

Lydia Sanderson has fled from a loveless, arranged marriage in which she was treated as little more than a field hand and source of sexual release. She tells her new friend, Evelyn Walker, "The truth is, I'd rather have my own house, sorry as it is, than the wedding ring of a dead man who couldn't be roused from sleeping when his own child was slipping out of me unborn." Tom Kromer's narrator never finds the economic security he seeks, but neither does he give up. His narration sings a song of inequality, cruelty, and deprivation precisely because he seeks—and knows he deserves— equality, human kindness, the chance to make a decent life. James Weldon Johnson's narrator lives a life of duplicity that is the radically unfair price of his own heritage. Johnson's narrator feels this injustice deep in bones and bristles against it; he knows better.

At the end of Hurston's *Their Eyes Were Watching God*, Jamie Crawford is accused of killing her husband—and she has in fact shot him to spare him the end stages of dying with rabies. In her defense at trial, "She made them [the jury] see she couldn't ever want to be rid of him. She didn't plead to anybody. She just sat there and told and when she was through she hushed." Janie Crawford believes in her own agency. And the jury, inevitably an all-white jury, believes her. Later, she tells her friend, "Love is lak de sea. It's uh moving thing, but still and all, it takes its shape from de shore it meets, and it's different with every shore." And ". . . two thing everybody's got tuh do fuh theyselves. They got tuh go tuh God, and they got tuh find out about livin' fuh theyselves."

Here's what teaching such novels has taught me: all means all. It means that that set of assumptions extolled in the Declaration of Independence extends to people of any skin color, people of any ethnicity, people of any gender identification or sexual orientation, people of any economic circumstance. All means all. Simply by being alive in the world we, each and all, have the right to expect and to claim those inalienable rights, rights which also impose obligations. As Janie says, some things ". . . everybody's got tuh do fuh theyselves."

However imperfectly the American effort has been heretofore (and it has been very far from perfect, as essentially all of the works of literature that I have taught have dramatized and made clear), I have nevertheless been comforted by the chance to engage these works in classrooms with other smart people. Together we have tried to understand and critique the gap between those American aspirations and the American reality—however large that gap has been. Though these novels make clear political implications, they are not in themselves political statements; they are so much more than that. Their most profound implications affirm what being human is. They reject cruelty, bigotry, and narcissism. Now living in what can only be called "the Trump era," I find myself, of necessity, going back to such works of literature, works that affirm and teach me yet about the intricacies of human experience, works that at their core (and imperfect as they are) encourage each reader to be better in action, deeper in thought, surer in the convictions of what it means to be one person among many.

Let the last quoted words here come from Lydia Sanderson. They can seem naïve now, even as they half do to Lydia herself: "'I had it in mind to come West and take up ranching.' She meant to keep out any sound of childishness, of foolish romanticism, though some of that had inspirited her once . . . . 'I suppose I was seeking the boundless possibilities that are said to live on the frontier.'"

When we read such American novels, that historically fraught frontier transforms. It becomes an American question: given inalienable human rights, how do we live, with each other, in freedom?

Works Cited

In order of publication:

The Autobiography of an Ex-Coloured Man, by James Weldon Johnson, Vintage edition 1989, first published by Alfred A. Knopf, 1927.

Waiting for Nothing, by Tom Kromer, American Century Series edition 1968, first published by Alfred A. Knopf, 1935.

Their Eyes Were Watching God, by Zora Neale Hurston, Perennial Library edition 1990, first published by J. B. Lippincott, Inc., 1937.

The Jump-Off Creek, by Molly Gloss, Houghton Mifflin Co., Boston, 1989.

"Where Are You From?"
An interview with Tina Schumann, editor of the anthology, *Two Countries: U.S. Daughters & Sons of Immigrant Parents*
by Sydney J. Elliott

> Skin had hope, that's what skin does.
> Heals over the scarred place, makes a road.
> Love means you breathe in two countries.
> And skin remembers—
>> "Two Countries," Naomi Shihab Nye

I wanted to begin this review with a pithy, thoughtful musing on the timeliness of this anthology. But I keep coming back to the simple fact that I can't stop picking up this book. I have gone back to essays such as Angie Chuang's essay, "Six Syllables," Li-Young Lee's poem, "Arise, Go Down," and the poem with the best title by Melissa Castillo-Garsow, "Poem To The White Man Who Asks Me After Overhearing Me Speak Spanish Where To Find The Best Mexican Food And Then Is Shocked To Find Out I Am Mexican." Nearly every page has pencil marks in the margins, underlines, and stars (which is my code for loving a line or section).

At the same time, this is an important and timely book. Tina Schumann brings together an anthology of poetry, essays, and flash memoir that highlight the immigrant experience from the voices of children growing up in America. In her introduction, Tina writes about living with the perpetual question, "Where are you from?" and our cultural impulse to categorize individuals even though ". . . the only box we all fit into is that of a human being."

Each writer in *Two Countries* shares a heritage statement to accompany their work, which are, to me, as interesting as the writing itself. The anthology, as a whole, successfully celebrates pride and culture as well as highlighting the human experience we all share.

Tina and I graduated from the same MFA program, the Rainier Writing Workshop at Pacific Lutheran University, so I approached her with some questions about *Two Countries*:

Sydney Elliott: You give your heritage story at the beginning in your introduction. How did the idea for this anthology germinate? How did you get started?

Tina Schumann: I suppose in some ways a seed of the idea had been germinating with me since childhood, but I became much more conscious of it in middle-age, after the death of my mother. I was lucky in that I came of age (mostly) in a very ethnically diverse neighborhood in the Bay Area in the 1970's. Most of my friends had one or more immigrant parent and English was not the only language spoken in their homes. My family was not seen as that unusual. As I grew into adulthood and moved around geographically, I recognized that many "American" families did not have that experience, and there were many instances in my life when I was treated as "other" once it was revealed that my mother was from El Salvador.

I wanted to know what that experience was like for other adult children of immigrants. Once I entered an MFA program in my 40's and began to see that many of my mentors and cohorts had edited anthologies on topics of interest to them I started to take the idea more seriously. I began the process in November of 2012 by posting a call for submissions in Poets & Writers magazine as well as a few other venues, such as DUOTROPE and CRWROPPS. I created a Gmail account for submissions and a blog page to post progress. I knew from the beginning that I wanted to include personal essays, flash memoir, and poetry. I am primarily a poet myself, but I am a huge consumer of memoir in my personal reading choices. So, I knew the value of including prose. I also knew early on that I would consider previously published material, as there were a few pieces I had my eye on, such as the poem "Two-Countries" by Naomi Shihab Nye and a few by Richard Blanco and Li-Young Lee.

As the submission process progressed, I was overwhelmed with the quality and quantity of submissions I received. I had to close submissions by April 2013. Being a novice to this process, I had no idea how many contributors to an anthology was acceptable, if my anthology would eventually acquire a publisher, and if I would be able to include all the writers that I had accepted so far. Not to mention writers I intended to solicit myself. There are many "IF's" in the creation of an anthology. One must have faith in their subject and contributors. I made sure to stipulate all of this to the contributors, and most of them were very gracious and so very glad that someone had asked about their life experience. I formatted the anthology alphabetically by last name (after some dithering with myself on other formatting possibilities; by genre? by country of origin?) and soon began the process of approaching publishers according to their guidelines. A few of my mentors had mentioned that they saw the collections as having course adoption possibilities, and so I focused on University presses to start with. Luckily, AWP (Association for Writers & Writing Programs) was taking place in Seattle in 2014, and so I made the rounds in the book fair handing out an engaging and descriptive flyer I had created regarding the availability and summary

> *The anthology, as a whole, successfully celebrates pride and culture as well as highlighting the human experience we all share.*

of the anthology. The University of New Mexico Press (UNMP) showed interest soon after, and we participated in a kind of editorial dance for the next two years. Ultimately, UNMP did not take the anthology, but the experience was invaluable to me as a first-time editor. I am very grateful to Red Hen Press for ultimately publishing the anthology in October of 2017. They are a hard working team and a dream to work with.

SE: What limitations or challenges did you encounter?

TS: Many of the challenges and limitations I encountered along the way were unknown to me in the beginning. They revealed themselves as the process went along. The first limitation I discovered was that I was limiting myself in my initial idea of the kind of writers and life experiences I thought I was after. I naively thought I would get material from writers whose experiences directly mirrored mine. That is, a writer born and raised in the U.S. from one or more immigrant parents. I quickly learned that there were many submissions from writers who were immigrants themselves but were brought to the U.S. at a very early age, and so they self-identified as more "American" than their parents. Writers like William Archila, Ocean Vuong, Mohja Kahf, Bunkong Tuon, and more, all born outside the U.S., but raised in the U.S. In response, I quickly revised the guidelines. The central theme of the anthology was to illustrate the many ways in which the children of immigrants came up against unique situations and were able to identify the many dichotomies between how their parents viewed the world and how they did as the result of coming of age in another country and under different cultural norms.

Some of the other challenges have to do with the logistics of curating, editing, and production details of the collection as a whole. This includes the solicitation process to certain publishers and writers, buying the rights to certain pieces of work and getting all seventy contributors to sign and return their author release forms in ink! (sounds simple, but I assure you it is not). Having to meticulously read and review each piece of material submitted several times, as well as heritage statements and bios and hope that I did not overlook some detail (which, by the way, even with the publisher's very smart editors meticulous reading over everything several times as well is still

I almost burst into tears when he asked me this as I had tried several different ways of getting ahold of Li-Young Lee, and it was starting to seem impossible.

going to happen.) The list goes on, even finding cover art that I liked, the press liked, and the distributor liked, turned into a bit of a challenge, but really all challenges were taken care of in the end, and nothing that could not be learned from, understood with good will from all, and ultimately, resulting in a collection that all parties are pleased with.

SE: I am amazed by the array of talent. The anthology contains well-known writers and poets as well as some wonderful new names. Some of the poets, in particular, are my writing idols. Was it daunting to approach some of these well-known writers? Or did they come to you?

TS: The majority of the collection contains writers that submitted their material to me via the submission process. There were a few writers in particular that I knew I would love to have in the collection, and I approached individually. It was a bit intimidating, but I was determined to try.

Tina Schumann and her book, Two Countries.

One of the writers I solicited was Naomi Shihab Nye, whose publisher sent me her email upon request. I then emailed her, explained the anthology and the poems I had in mind and she kindly agreed all in the same day. She is really a gem of a human being. Another was Richard Blanco, whose agent I contacted via his website about a week after he read at Obama's second inauguration. We got a dialog going and then he seemed unreachable for several months. Luckily, that same year, I spotted Richard in the hallway at AWP, and I practically tackled him (which for me is quite the overt gesture.) I explained the anthology, my wishes to include his work and he graciously agreed as well. I lucked out on getting work from Li-Young Lee as I was in negotiation with the company that holds the rights to Joseph Legaspi's work, and the agent just happened to ask me if I would be interested in any work by Li-Young Lee because they held the rights to his works as well. I almost burst into tears when he asked me this as I had tried several different ways of getting ahold of Li-Young Lee, and it was starting to seem impossible. So that was a small miracle.

Ira Sukrungruang had a personal essay in Brevity that I loved called "Chop Suey," and I had gotten to know Ira over the years, so I asked him for that. I also asked Mohja Kahf for her incredible poem I came across online called "My Grandmother Washes Her Feet in the Sink of the Bathroom at Sears." Prageeta Sharma and Kazim Ali were both also very generous in allowing us to reprint their poems as well. I feel lucky in that Ocean Vuong's work was the second submission I received back in 2012 before his career really took off. He did not have a full collection out at that time. I remember thinking when I read his submission, "Wow, this kid is really special." Turns out he was and is! If I was editing this collection today, he would be someone whose work I would solicit. Luckily, I did not have to.

Protest signs in Seattle, Washington.

A few things I learned from soliciting the work of others is that just because the author verbally gives you their approval (or even submitted their material) to reprint their work that does not mean it is a done deal. Their publisher will need to approve it, most likely have a legal form for you and your publisher to sign, and possibly expect some kind of monetary compensation for the reprint as well as a guaranteed free copy of the anthology to the author. Again, a challenge but not unachievable.

SE: In your introduction, you write, "Children trapped between the desperation of adult lives, politics, economics, conceptual borders and the realization that a bright future may not be available to them on either side of the border." I'm only guessing that this project started before our current administration, travel bans, and border walls. Do you feel that this anthology, these voices, may be more important than ever in finding a sense of humanity or being a voice to those who don't have one at this time?

TS: It is sadly serendipitous AND fortuitous that the anthology is appearing at this difficult time. When I began this anthology, President Obama was in the closing year of his first term. In fact, I mention him and Sonia Sotomayor, the Supreme Court justice whose parents are from Cuba in my introduction as two examples of the children of immigrants. I could not have imagined then in my wildest nightmares that we would be where weare now. I have mixed emotions about the collection's timely publication. I am both glad that the book appeared now and sad that I have to

Second Ellis Island Immigration Station, opened on December 17, 1900, as seen in 1905.

say that at all. Of course, my hope is that the collection will stand as further evidence that America was and always has been great because of immigrants. Any American you meet is here because at some point an ancestor made the arduous journey here from somewhere else. Look far enough back in anyone's family history and you will find an immigrant (whether by force or free will.) What makes one person's journey and dreams more legitimate than any others? Every human being is a human being first, with all the same rights to life, liberty and the pursuit of happiness.

I do not delude myself into believing that the narrow-minded segment of our population in this country who would truly benefit from reading this anthology will buy it or check it out of the library or go to a reading. But I will allow myself to hope that possibly, just possibly, the contributors and I have done our part to represent those that cannot speak for themselves and to show our strength in numbers, in works of art and in stories that illustrate the best of America and the best of humanity.

Poems
by Oliver de la Paz

Meditation with Smoke and Flowers

It is Monday and I am not thinking of myself. My son, asleep
in his stroller, the dark conifers holding nothing but their scent.

I'm walking him to the place where loggers have cleared thirty acres,
leaving only ash and stripped tree limbs. The light now comes

to the places once dark—and now wildflowers where once
the moss grew thick and complete. The flame of something around the corner

and I'm thinking of the wild tiger lilies that line this gravel road below my house,
how they clump together, their stems bent down from the weight

of their flowers. How mouth-like they are, and how
their speechlessness makes the road quieter. Each flower is a surprise,

like the flaming tip of cigarettes in the dark. I think that the road
cannot contain all these mouths, though there are mythologies held

in check by the tongue. Like the story my father told me
about his father in war time, and how his own father forced him, with the threat

of a beating, to go under the house for a cigarette from a Japanese foot soldier
bunkered down. I can see my father's small trembling hand,

outstretched to this man whose face is mud-caked, smelling
slightly of fire and lubricant for his rifle. The smoke from the soldier's own

cigarette takes the shape of the underside of the house and I imagine
my father can hear his own father above him pacing.

But this road now, is free of smoke. The logging trucks have taken off
for the night and the tree remnants have smoldered into nothing

but charcoal. The wreck of everything is a vacuum, so too the wreck of a village
after war or the floor boards above a son's head in fear of his own father.

Here, though, there is nothing to fear. The wheels of the stroller on gravel
is the only sound and the idleness of the excavation trucks harkens to

someone asleep in the uneasy dark. No, I am not thinking of myself. I'm thinking
of an agreement my father must have made with himself years ago

when the houses were burning into bright bouquets in the nighttime. How, perhaps
he swore he would not beat his own son while somewhere in the afterlife his own father

smokes and paces. Perhaps there are no flowers in that place. Perhaps
the lone soldier through with hiding, crawled out after the guns had stopped

and dusted himself off, the sun striking his face with its unreasonable light.
I'm thinking of my son, asleep, and of the wild tiger lilies. How frail they are

in the new light. Why they come. Why they spring up, unannounced
as suddenly as the promises we make with ourselves when we are young.

In Defense of Small Towns

When I look at it, it's simple, really. I hated life there. September,
once filled with animal deaths and toughened hay. And the smells

of Fall were boiled down beets and potatoes
or the farmhands' breeches smeared with oil and diesel

as they rode into town, dusty and pissed. The radio station
split time between metal and Tejano, and the only action

happened on Friday nights where the high school football team
gave everyone a chance at forgiveness. The town left no room

for novelty or change. The sheriff knew everyone's son and despite that,
we'd cruise up and down the avenues, switching between

brake and gearshift. We'd fight and spit chew into Big Gulp cups
and have our hearts broken nightly. In that town I learned

to fire a shotgun at nine and wring a chicken's neck
with one hand by twirling the bird and whipping it straight like a towel.

But I loved the place once. Everything was blonde and cracked
and the irrigation ditches stretched to the end of the earth. You could

ride on a bicycle and see clearly, the outline of every leaf
or catch on the streets, each word of a neighbor's argument.

Nothing could happen there and if I willed it, the place would have me
slipping over its rocks into the river with the sugar plant's steam

or signing papers at a storefront army desk, buttoned up
with medallions and a crew cut, eyeing the next recruits.

If I've learned anything, it's that I could be anywhere,
staring at a hunk of asphalt or listening to the clap of billiard balls

against each other in a bar and hear my name. Indifference now?
Some. I shook loose, but that isn't the whole story. The fact is

I'm still in love. And when I wake up, I watch my son yawn
and my mind turns his upswept hair into cornstalks

at the edge of a field. Stillness is an acre, and his body
idles, deep like heavy machinery. I want to take him back there,

to the small town of my youth and hold the book of wildflowers
open for him, and look. I want him to know the colors of horses,

to run with a cattail in his hand and watch as its seeds
fly weightless as though nothing mattered, as though

the little things we tell ourselves about our pasts stay there,
rising slightly and just out of reach.

"Meditation with Smoke and Flowers" and "In Defense of Small Towns" appear in the collection *Requiem for the Orchard* by Oliver De la Paz (University of Akron Press). They also appear in the anthology, *Two Countries: U.S. Daughters and Sons of Immigrant Parents* (Red Hen Press). Reprint permissions from the author.

Haunted Shores
by Julie Leung

As I joined other volunteer beach naturalists at the shore for an evening walk, I wondered whether we would find live starfish or only dead ones. On the first Monday night in December 2013, I had hiked to the beach beside the Bainbridge Island ferry terminal, numb fingers clumsily handling flashlight and phone, tired eyes straining to see through the darkness. During the summer, the extreme low tides in Puget Sound occurred during daylight hours, but in winter, the low tides happened at night.

I had first learned about tides when my parents separated and my grandmother invited us to visit her. Each summer after the divorce, my mother drove her four children to the Oregon coast, where I counted hundreds of starfish, *Pisaster ochraceus*, clustered and contorted together, as I climbed barefoot over exposed rocks and imagined I, too, could grow tube feet and become a tenacious creature of the tides. These large stars were not the fragile foil stickers of school charts, instead they had strong and sturdy bodies like athletes with impressive rays that twisted into artistic curves. After months of staring at sterile hospital walls during my younger brother's illness, I had delighted in the purple and orange hues of *Pisaster*, the magenta reds of scurrying crabs, and the neon greens of sticky anemones, brighter than the colors of candies and popsicles.

But in the beam of my flashlight on this December Monday night, the beach appeared dull, like the faded photographs from my 1980s childhood, revealing mostly grays. Instead of my childhood beach attire of shorts and T-shirt or my favorite rainbow-striped one-piece swimsuit, I wore two pairs of wool socks inside clunky rubber boots, "alpine" synthetic outdoor pants, and an old coat zippered over a fleece jacket and a wool sweater. A knit hat with a brim sheltered my headlamp and the glasses that strengthened my contacts prescription for night driving, allowing me to see. My legs ached after clomping in boots, and since my nose had become congested from the cold, I had lost my ability to smell. I resembled an awkward mix of geek, gardener, and REI, a species native only to Pacific Northwest shores. I began to wonder why I had come.

In the five years since I had taken beach naturalist training classes, I had never attended a night beach walk. But this fall, starfish, or sea stars, as they were also called by scientists, had suffered a mysterious illness, named Sea Star Wasting Syndrome. In a video, I had gasped while watching a sick star spinning in a tank, rays detaching one at a time, like an amusement park ride turned nightmare, until the animal was armless and dead. Or the sea stars shriveled and "melted" into "goo". Images of emaciated echinoderms and their white ghostly remains had haunted my computer screen for months. Although I preferred to be warm and at home with my family on a winter night, resting beneath blankets, I wanted to see starfish one more time before they disappeared.

Monday, December 2, was also the day after World AIDS Day. Before packing my phone into my coat pocket, I had read a link from Facebook to an article on Gao Yaojie, "The AIDS Granny," a gynecologist who discovered the Chinese government had been failing to protect people in the blood transfusions and donation systems. Despite denials and deception, she had continued to speak and donate her pension and savings to AIDS victims. After she was placed under house arrest, she escaped to New York.

I couldn't remember exactly when I first heard of AIDS or HIV. But I remembered the fear. I was a young teenager. Could I get HIV from sitting on a toilet seat? Kissing a boy? But I wanted a boy to kiss me. What about sharing a Cherry Coke with friends? Sex and needles were proven modes of transmission. I hadn't had sex or used drugs. But scientists

These large stars were not the fragile foil stickers of school charts, instead they had strong and sturdy bodies like athletes with impressive rays that twisted into artistic curves.

didn't seem to have all the answers about AIDS or understand all the transmission possibilities. It could take months to seroconvert after contracting the virus. Could you get AIDS from going to the dentist? A young woman claimed she had. Rock Hudson died from AIDS. My mother was surprised. But Ryan White, a teenager my age, had AIDS. So did a blond mom named Elizabeth. Both of them died. HIV infection was mysterious and lethal. Anyone could get AIDS. No one had a cure.

During the summers I was seventeen, eighteen, and nineteen, I worked in a large hospital laboratory in Seattle, using serum samples, leftover blood taken from patients, to compare two different tests for an enzyme. Labels in neon yellow and pink marked some of the patient tubes, urging precautions. Researchers informed me that these blood samples probably contained HIV. I wore gloves, a coat, and a disposable paper facemask. Each time I pipetted patient serum, I wondered if I could catch HIV, if the blood splashed in my eye, up my nose, or contacted my skin, unseen. It seemed possible that AIDS could be transmitted in other ways not yet understood. Once a week I attended microbiology rounds where we passed petri dishes with cultures of patient blood and bodily fluids, even opening and sniffing them to help confirm the diagnoses. At a presentation, I learned about Karposi's sarcoma, visible as lesions on the skin, a secondary infection common with HIV, listed as a cause of death for many AIDS patients.

Six months after my final laboratory summer, in early 1991, I asked my boyfriend to drive me to the anonymous HIV testing clinic near our university. We had started to discuss our future, but I wanted to get tested before we made deeper commitments to each other. The chances were small and I had taken precautions, but HIV infection was not impossible. If I went to the doctor, the results would be forever in my file, so I chose anonymous testing. After giving blood, I took my number home on a piece of paper. I counted the days until I could call. Pressing my phone to my ear, I stood at my desk, by my third-floor dorm room window beneath the campus clock, overlooking the courtyard, speaking my number into the receiver. Waiting for the reply. Negative. I was HIV negative. I exhaled and called my boyfriend. How long did I wait for results? At least two or three days. A weekend? I don't remember. It seemed forever. Whenever I see my own blood spurting from a cut or flowing into a tube outside my body, I remember those long days.

My summers in the large hospital lab fit into my plan to pursue a career in medical research. After watching my brother's struggle with cancer, I wanted to cure, to help, to heal. Yet later, as a young adult, I felt deficient and frustrated. I struggled in college science and math classes. While shadowing a hospital surgeon, I realized I didn't have the stoicism required for medicine, and while working in an immunology lab for a few years, I learned I lacked the intensity and personality needed to pursue a PhD. Instead I studied nonprofit management and then stayed home with children.

At her home, she showed me a documentary that had aired on TV: the men walking and holding hands in the past, the lover's gray gravesite now.

Living in California, a few years after my test, I met a new friend whose brother was HIV positive. His lover had died from AIDS. At her home, she showed me a documentary that had aired on TV: the men walking and holding hands in the past, the lover's gray gravesite now. My friend and her brother helped care for AIDS patients in San Francisco. I wanted to join them but I felt too timid and too distant from the huge city. Although I lost contact with my friend after moving from California, I found a recent YouTube video where her brother wondered why he has survived so many years, living decades with HIV and AIDS, while his lover and many friends have died.

At the ferry terminal, I could see beams of flashlights illuminating circles of gray sand and the line of Seattle skyscrapers on the horizon, nine miles to the east across this estuary named Puget Sound, a mix of Pacific Ocean and mountain rivers. Two volunteers were already searching, and soon more arrived. In the dark, I recognized some but others were strangers. Many volunteers were retirees and I often was the youngest one.

My flashlights soon frustrated me. While rushing to leave the house, I had grabbed a headlamp used only once a year on our annual camping weekend and a small flashlight from the kitchen junk drawer. I had considered hauling the Coleman lantern but decided it was too heavy and too bright. On the beach, I realized that my headlamp was difficult and inefficient to control under my hat. My gloved fingers couldn't press the buttons well in the cold and I constantly needed to adjust the angle to avoid blinding people moving near me. The beam on my flashlight was weak. But it was what I had.

Walking as a group, we admired the "shaggy mouse" sea slugs and sharp-nosed crabs in the shallow waves. Then, on the sand, I saw white outlines of stars. The sickness.

When sea stars started dying this fall along the West Coast from Alaska to California, scientists across the country quickly collaborated to research the disease. Divers had first noticed ill sea stars in Vancouver B.C. but within weeks the disease had also been observed in Seattle. "They've sent specimens to Cornell," said one naturalist in our group as we looked at the animals "melting" on the shore, their bodies oozing and dissolving. I thought I found a sea cucumber, and I thought I had found a sea slug. Looking closer, I realized they both were remnants of star bodies split apart by wasting.

Pisaster ochraceus.

"Here's one of the last living specimens," called one of the naturalists as we walked under the ferry terminal. We aimed our flashlights on a scarlet sunflower star, *Pycnopodia helianthoides*, as wide as my forearm, with twenty rays, like slender petals.

"Let's be optimistic." I said.

A few years ago, sunflower stars had crowded the shores of the island during the spring low tides, circles in the vibrant colors of sunsets, soft to touch when I stroked one with a finger. In my childhood explorations of Cannon Beach, I knew the rigid and sturdy *Pisaster* on the rocks, but I had never seen the soft *Pycnopodia* until I moved to Bainbridge Island. Sunflower stars are among the largest and fastest echinoderms in the world. A friend walking the beach with me gasped to see these animals in red, orange, and purple velveteen: "I've only seen them on TV!" I didn't remember seeing *Pycnopodi*a on TV, but they were worthy of prime time. Speed of one meter per second. Diameter of one meter in size. Tens of thousands of cream-colored tube feet. I had wondered if the celebrity creature was from another world.

Falling stars, white fireworks, appeared to the south, probably celebrating a win by the Seahawks. I hoped my children had turned off the TV and gone to bed.

Under the ferry terminal, I touched a *Pycnopodia* the color of a Creamsicle. It felt slimy not firm. It was not moving. Another chocolate-colored sunflower star appeared to be melting. We found at least five or six that could be healthy. My photos were blurs, lines of lights in motion, reminding me of astronomy images, as if I was trying to take a picture of stars at night while the earth moved. I was too cold to hold still long enough to focus. We walked beneath concrete, circling our lights to see the healthy and the sick.

As we stared at sea star remains, a voice in the darkness, an older man in the group, someone I didn't know, said, "Imagine what will happen when something hits us and no one can figure it out."

I left the beach after an hour, needing to check on my children at home. We volunteers had gathered together that night to save sea stars, not to interrogate each other. But I wanted to yell at this stranger. I wanted to tell him we didn't need to "imagine." Had he forgotten the '80s and '90s? Rock Hudson? Ryan White? Had he ever watched his blood slowly fill a tube or had he ever pressed the phone against his ear until it hurt, fearing results? Had he ever lost someone he loved, as mystified doctors stood by, unable to help? Retrovirals and new prophylactic medications had increased survival rates, reducing the danger of HIV infection and the mortality of AIDS, at least in the United States, I understood, after reading articles in *The New York Times*. But zoonoses such as SARS, and influenzas including H5N1 bird flu and H1N1 swine flu have troubled the twenty-first century. Mysterious epidemics would continue to "hit" us.

Our polluted planet may no longer be able to sustain human life in a generation or two, I've also read. Climate change, ocean acidification, and plastic waste have impacted our world. Turning on NPR, I often heard discussions on extinction. All life on earth was fragile. "Ashes to ashes, dust to dust," I heard as a child.

"Do unto others as you would have them do to you," I had also heard in childhood. Didn't the Golden Rule also apply to purple and ochre stars?

Four weeks later, on December 30, the last Monday night in December, I stood again on the edge of Puget Sound with volunteer naturalists. A researcher from the national collaboration had traveled to Bainbridge Island to teach citizen scientists how to monitor sea stars and participate in the research. I'd brought the headlamp since the email invitation from our coordinator had

Big Sur, California.

mentioned headlamps, and I'd grabbed a larger flashlight from my car, hoping it would provide better light. This night, slightly warmer, I chose to go without gloves, although I kept the layers of coats and the rubber boots.

Before we examined the tide pools, the dozen of us stood in a circle beside our cars in the parking strip of Rockaway Beach, while the researcher, a professor, shared what he knew, speaking in the darkness, as if telling ghost stories. Sea stars had been ill in the past but usually only in California. After contracting the wasting disease, these echinoderms had died from secondary bacterial infections. Transmission had been unclear. Local environmental factors including water temperature and sewer outfall could be important. Shipping could also have helped spread the pathogen: large port cities such as Vancouver, B.C. and Seattle had shown more illness than smaller towns. People had wondered if Fukushima, the Japanese nuclear reactor disaster, could be responsible but scientists so far did not have any evidence. Humans had not become ill after touching sick sea stars. But we should rinse our boots and equipment with bleach water or fresh water between beaches in order to minimize transmission.

The sky was clear, an exceptional winter night in the Northwest. I noticed the constellation of Orion the hunter above us, as we started our own hunt, looking for sea stars. I remembered atoms on this beach, in our bodies, in the rocks, in the water, and in these animals, all once belonged to the stars.

Our group walked across the beach of noisy cobbles in the dark, helping each other with flashlights and hands to cross over the wobbling stones. At the tide pools, the researcher demonstrated how to look for lesions, areas of white contrasting on the orange and purple of *Pisaster*. Four times a year we citizen scientists would measure the length of the sea star rays and categorize their levels of illness. With flashlights, we took turns learning how to bend plastic rulers across each sea star's rays,

so we could read and record numbers. Later, at home, I would find blood on a finger, only noticing then that I had ripped my skin across the barnacled rocks in the dark. Again, my headlamp felt awkward to control, as I continually adjusted the angle and brightness, so I turned it off. The large yellow flashlight from my car seemed a better choice even though it appeared dimmer on the beach than I had imagined.

In one tide pool, a sea star had disintegrated into a disturbing stew: a mix of purple skin with remnants of white and orange organs. The researcher explained that in general when animals were ill, they could reabsorb their gonads to help them survive. But with the rapid progression of sea star wasting disease, the orange gonads ruptured and dissolved, and the dying animal transformed into a soup of white and orange.

Next, we walked back to cars and drove to Point White, a long dock on the south side of the island, once the site of a small ferry terminal last century but now used by teenagers for summer dives and dares. At low tides, we often would find *Pisaster ochraceus* decorating the dock pilings with a tessellating carpet of colors and stars. I had last visited Point White for a beach walk we had held in the spring, a sunny day where we had found for the first time a sand star, *Luidia foliolata*, an elegant, gray, five-rayed echinoderm. But as we arrived under the dock in the December darkness, we discovered only mussels, barnacles, and sea slugs on the piers. Other naturalists had observed more echinoderms on the dock only a few weeks earlier. Sea stars had disappeared. "This is sad," I repeated as I inspected the pilings, ignoring my aching feet and poor vision.

On the south side of one pier we found a cluster of a half dozen purple *Pisaster*, but some were ill. Wading into the waves, we measured the ray length, the radius of these ochre sea stars. I stretched a plastic ruler across the star bodies, feeling the rigid, bumpy surface of the "spiny skinned" echinoderms. Some were 250 millimeters, larger than the charts, others only 10 mm, tinier than my thumbnail. One large sea star appeared stressed and ill, attached by only two arms, its body lumpy, the other arms pulled away. During our time under the dock, this animal fell into the water. Inside a rotten piling, detached arms dissolved into white "goo," indicating illness. Rays lay scattered across the beach. Someone corrected my counts, showing me tiny sea stars I had missed on a piling. After three hours, my hands were numb and dirty, my feet felt cold, and I worried that the rising waves of the returning tide would soon spill into my boots.

Why had I come to the beach on December nights, trudging in thick boots through cold darkness? As a young girl in hospital waiting rooms, I believed that I too could become ill with incurable cancer, like my brother wrapped in white bandages. As a teen, I knew I could be infected with HIV. Through biology studies, I learned that only random atoms, different bits of DNA, separated me from my sick brother, and even from sea stars and anemones. Life, in its glorious oranges and purples, in the rigidity of *Pisaster* and softness of *Pycnopodia*, in the scurrying of crabs and tenacity of tube feet, needed to be experienced, protected, nurtured, and celebrated whenever the tide allowed.

"In my view," Gao Yaojie said, "one should not live simply for himself or herself but should think of others. An owl is born to eat mice, and a dragonfly is born to eat mosquitoes. Man should be also born to do something."

As I have become older, I have longed for more boldness, wanting to ignore my doubts and inadequacies, and instead explore and love.

After arriving at home, I posted a photo of a sea star lesion on my Facebook page, white emerging on a purple echinoderm. "Isn't there something we can do?" commented one of my friends. The next day, my youngest child shared at a New Year's Eve party that sea stars were turning into goo, but the other kids laughed and didn't believe her.

Before leaving, we examined the beach beside the pier. Tiny shrimp darted in the flashlight beams. Someone found a stranded fish the size of a finger and carried it back to the water where it seemed to swim away. We saw a few healthy sea stars but no sand stars. One of the volunteers asked the researcher about his flashlight. It was a diver's light. He said he had learned he would see more if he had a good light.

I wanted to see more. I have always wanted to see more, know more, understand more, and love more, with whatever time and atoms I have. As I have become older, I have longed for more boldness, wanting to ignore my doubts and inadequacies, and instead explore and love. The many mysteries of our planet amaze me. Amidst the horrors, epidemics have revealed the interdependency and complexity of life, the fragility of our stardust bodies, the need for empathy, compassion, and faith.

"I need to walk back with someone who has a light," another naturalist asked, explaining her battery had died. Sure, I said. Though the beam was weak, I aimed my light as best I could, circles on the sand showing us where to take the next step.

Ursula K. Le Guin. Copyright © by Marian Wood Kolisch.

"A writer is a person who cares what words mean, what they say, how they say it. Writers know words are their way towards truth and freedom, and so they use them with care, with thought, with fear, with delight. By using words well they strengthen their souls. Story-tellers and poets spend their lives learning that skill and art of using words well. And their words make the souls of their readers stronger, brighter, deeper.

—**Ursula K. Le Guin**

Contributors

Andrew Bishop is Coordinator of Composition II at Hudson County Community College in Jersey City, NJ, where he teaches courses in composition and literature. In 2017, he was an NEH Summer Scholar studying "Transcendentalism and Reform," and his reflections on teaching Thoreau in an urban setting have recently been published in *The Concord Saunterer*. He has an article on "Wasted Bulls and Fungus-Ridden Fish" forthcoming in *The Hemingway Review*. In 2016, he attended the TYCA Northeast Regional Conference, where he presented a version of the paper published in this journal. His M.A. in English is from the University of Tennessee, Knoxville.

Sydney J. Elliott graduated from Pacific Lutheran University's Rainer Writing Workshop in 2015. She is a full-time English instructor at Tillamook Bay Community College and lives on the Oregon coast. She is the editor of the *Community College Humanities Review* and serves as the Community College Humanities Association's National Publications Director. Sydney is also a surfer, yoga instructor, self-defense teacher, and singer in a jazz trio.

Sunithi Gnanadoss earned her Master of Arts in English from The University of Madras, India. She is currently working on her PhD on Theorizing Indian Immigrant Feminism: A Study of Indian Immigrant Novels. Sunithi has taught college in India, made a brief foray into High School teaching in America, and has been a member of the English Faculty at Germanna Community College since 2004. She led two study abroad programs to India. She won the Richard Gossweiler award for Teaching Excellence which came with grant to support research of a topic in the Humanities. This led to her pursuit in the feminist research on Indian Immigrant Literature. She is currently using the Orange Education Grant to promote multicultural discussion titled: *The American Dream: A Quilt of Conflicting Patterns.*

Julie Jeanell Leung received her MFA from the Rainier Writing Workshop at Pacific Lutheran University. Her creative nonfiction has appeared in a number of publications, including the *Bellingham Review, Blue Lyra Review, and Grist: The Journal for Writers*. A beach naturalist and citizen scientist, Julie lives with her family on Bainbridge Island where she counts sea stars on the rocky shores.

Oliver de la Paz is the author of four collections of poetry: *Names Above Houses, Furious Lullaby, Requiem for the Orchard* (winner of the Akron Prize for poetry chosen by Martin Espada), and *Post Subject: A Fable.* He is the coeditor with Stacey Lynn Brown of *A Face to Meet the Faces: An Anthology of Contemporary Persona Poetry.* He co-chairs the advisory board of Kundiman, a not-for-profit organization dedicated to the promotion of Asian American Poetry, and serves on the Association of Writers and Writing Programs Board of Trustees. A recipient of a NYFA Fellowship Award and a GAP Grant from Artist Trust, he has published work in journals such as *Virginia Quarterly Review, North American Review, Tin House,* and *Chattahoochee Review,* and in anthologies such as *Asian American Poetry: The Next Generation* and *Two Countries: U.S. Daughters and Sons of Immigrant Parents.* He teaches at the College of the Holy Cross and in the Low-Residency MFA Program at Pacific Lutheran University.

John Pruitt is Associate Professor of English at the University of Wisconsin-Rock County and Editor of *Wisconsin English Journal.* His scholarship on teaching and learning has appeared in journals such as *College English* and *Teaching English in the Two-Year College,* and his book *Curricular Innovations: LGBT Literature and the New English Studies,* co-edited with William P Banks, is forthcoming from Peter Lang.

Andrew Rusnak Jr. was a stringer for several weeklies while earning a B.S. in English from Towson University. He was employed by the aerospace industry as a technical writer for 10 years before returning to journalism where he covered the White House, Capitol Hill, Congress, the Environmental Protection Agency and the Department of Energy, writing on environmental remediation technologies, renewable energy, and nuclear and hazardous waste cleanup. As communications director for several Washington, D.C. associations, he edited trade magazines and peer reviewed journals (print and online), managed websites and online content strategies, and conducted media and public relations campaigns. He has a Master's in Liberal Arts and the History of Ideas from The Johns Hopkins University, a Master's in Liberal Studies from Loyola University, and a Master's in Writing from The Johns Hopkins University. He teaches contextualized composition (STEM, Creative Nonfiction, Reportage) at the Community College of Baltimore County. He also serves as Executive Director of the CCHA.

Lex Runciman, Linfield College professor emeritus of English, has published six collections of poems, including *The Admirations*, which won the Oregon Book Award. His new and selected poems, *Salt Moons: Poems 1981-2016*, was published earlier this year by Salmon Poetry. The chapter discussing his work concludes Erik Muller's new book, *Durable Goods: Appreciations of Oregon Poets*. Runciman was the first in his family to graduate from college. He earned his master's degree from the University of Montana, where he studied with Madeline DeFrees and Richard Hugo, and his Ph.D. from the University of Utah. He and his wife, Deborah Berry Runciman, have been married more than 40 years.

Tina Schumann is the author of three poetry collections: *As If* (Parlor City Press 2010), which was awarded the Stephen Dunn Poetry Prize; *Requiem. A Patrimony of Fugues* (Diode Editions 2016), which won the Diode Editions Chapbook Contest for 2016; and *Praising the Paradox* (Red Hen Press 2019), which was a finalist in the National Poetry Series, Four Way Books Intro Prize and the New Issues Poetry Prize. She curated and edited the anthology, *Two Countries. U.S. Daughters and Sons of Immigrant Parents* (Red Hen Press 2017). Schumann's work received the 2009 American Poet Prize from The American Poetry Journal, a pushcart nomination and finalist status in the 2013 Terrain.org Annual Poetry Contest, as well as honorable mention in *The Atlantic* poetry contest. She was a featured poet at the 2014 Skagit River Poetry Festival and is Assistant Director at Artsmith.org. Her poems have appeared in publications and anthologies including *The American Journal of Poetry, Ascent, Atticus Review, Cimarron Review, Midwest Quarterly, Nimrod, Parabola, Palabra, Tarrain.org, The Yale Journal for Humanities in Medicine* and *Verse Daily.*

Billy Tooma is the award-nominated filmmaker of the documentaries *Clarence Chamberlin: Fly First & Fight Afterward, Poetry of Witness*, and *The Black Eagle of Harlem*. He holds multiple degrees in literature and writing from William Paterson University and Drew University. Just recently he was awarded tenure and the rank of Assistant Professor at Essex County College.

Photo Credits

On Brutal Auditions, the Exigencies of Spring, and the Life of Professor Christopher Wolfe
Banner: Untitled (Clarinet) from profile 2204574. Commercial use.
  https://pixabay.com/en/clarinet-music-jazz-1780817
Portraits (1-2): Untitled (Christopher Wolfe), from Christopher Wolfe. Used with permission.
Clarinets (1): "clarinet" from MaZiKab. Commercial Use.
  https://stock.adobe.com/images/clarinet/198875211
Clarinets (2):"Klarinette auf einem Notenblatt" from GIBLEHO. Commercial use.
  https://stock.adobe.com/images/klarinette-auf-einem-notenblatt/62236873
Clarinets (3): "Dismantled Clarinet on a Black Table" from Ana-Maria Tegzes. Commercial use.
  https://stock.adobe.com/images/dismantled-clarinet-on-a-black-table/130245206
Clarinet (4): "Clarinet Bell on Old Writing Background" from Kris Black. Commercial use.
  https://stock.adobe.com/images/clarinet-bell-on-old-writing-background/83256711

Biography & Documentary: Academia's Evolution
Banner: Untitled (filming) from Sam McGhee. Commercial use.
  https://unsplash.com/photos/KieCLNzKoBo
Film: Untilted from profile 15299. Commercial use.
   https://pixabay.com/en/film-antique-8-mm-kodachrome-102681/
Camera: Untitled from Free-Photos. Commercial use.
  https://pixabay.com/en/camera-photography-lens-equipment-690163/
Popcorn: Untitled from Christian Wiediger. Commercial use.
  https://unsplash.com/photos/AEeoY_aqvNk
Reel: Untitled from JayMantri. Commercial use.
  https://pixabay.com/en/film-reel-movies-film-movie-438408/

A New School of Feminism: An Academic Exercise or an Ethnographic Reality?
Banner 1: The Goddess Lakshmi by Raja Ravi Varma. Public domain.
  https://en.wikipedia.org/wiki/Lakshmi#/media/File:Raja_Ravi_Varma,_Goddess_
  Lakshmi,_1896.jpg
Draupadi: The Disrobing of Draupadi (painting), attributed to Nainsukh. Public domain.
  https://en.wikipedia.org/wiki/Mahabharata#/media/File:Disrobing_of_Draupadi.jpg

Teaching Literacy Through a Cultural Studies Approach to London
Banner: "Sapphire Eye" (London) from Garrett Brooks. Used with Permission.
Parliament: Untitled from Eva Dang. Commercial use.
  https://unsplash.com/photos/EXdXLrZXS9Q
Reading: Untitled from João Silas. Commercial use.
  https://unsplash.com/photos/9c_djeQTDyY
London: Untitled from Jaanus Jagomägi. Commercial use.
  https://unsplash.com/photos/Dymu1WiZVko
Lamp: Untitled from William Santos. Commercial use.
  https://unsplash.com/photos/0nnuhlN0BSY
Thames: Untitled from luxstorm. Commercial use.
  https://pixabay.com/en/bridge-london-westminster-898753/

Literary Cures for Common Sense Thinking in the Composition Classroom
Banner: Untitled (reader) by Ben White. Commercial use.
    https://unsplash.com/photos/1MHU3zpTvro
Books: Untitled by Alfons Morales. Commercial use.
    https://unsplash.com/photos/YLSwjSy7stw
Reader: Untitled from Maciej Ostrowski. Commercial use.
    https://unsplash.com/photos/MdeHq5ZD_Xw

All Means All
Banner: The Statue of Liberty from Fabian Fauth. Commercial use.
    https://unsplash.com/photos/1_EedIBc6jY
Book: Their Eyes Were Watching God by Zora Neale Hurston, from the Library of Congress.
    Public domain. http://www.loc.gov/exhibits/books-that-shaped-america/1900-1950/Assets/
    ba0056_enlarge.jpg

Where Are You From? A Conversation with Tina Schumann
Banner: Book cover. Used with permission.
Portrait: Tina Schumann. Used with permission.
Rally: Untitled Nitish Meena. Commercial use.
    https://unsplash.com/photos/IFh4o-U-BGg
Island: "Second Ellis Island Immigration Station" from the Library of Congress. Public domain.
    https://en.wikipedia.org/wiki/Ellis_Island#/media/File:Ellis_Island_in_1905.jpg

Poems: "Meditation with Smoke and Flowers" & "In Defense of Small Towns"
Banner: Untitled (tiger lily) from phoenix727. Commercial use.
    https://pixabay.com/en/lilium-lancifolium-lily-1599738/

Haunted Shores
Banner: Untitled (shore) from Aaron Burden. Commercial use.
    https://unsplash.com/photos/rdG4hRoyVR0
Starfish: Purple Starfish from Steve Voght. Commercial use.
    https://flic.kr/p/4yWyMS   https://creativecommons.org/licenses/by-sa/2.0
Beach: Untitled (Big Sur) from Kace Rodriguez. Commercial use.
    https://unsplash.com/photos/t_OUw49w3tM
Starfish: "Purple Sea Star" from Don Henise. Commercial use.
    https://flic.kr/p/nJhi9r   https://creativecommons.org/licenses/by/2.0/

Ursula K. Le Guin
Portrait: Copyright © by Marian Wood Kolisch.
    http://www.ursulakleguin.com/PublicityPhotos.html#Kolisch

CCHA Community College Humanities Association

JOIN TODAY

The Humanities: Education for a Lifetime

Today's students face professional lives that demand continual education in response to changing employment/career options, new advances in technology and an ever-changing world.

The humanities provide the best instruction in analyzing alternative possibilities and adapting to change, skills that are essential for continual personal and professional growth and education. The humanities help students understand culture, their own and that of others. The humanities help students learn how to think critically. To ensure this unique contribution to our students' education, the humanities need your support.

Your Role in CCHA

CCHA's mission requires the continuing support of its member and others who value the essential contributions of the humanities for today's students, both as individuals and as members of society. Individual CCHA membership unites you with your colleagues at two-year colleges across the nation in shaping and strengthening the humanities. Institutional CCHA membership makes a valuable contribution to the advancement of the humanities at two-year colleges.

Join or Renew with CCHA at:

www.cchumanities.org

Made in the USA
Columbia, SC
14 May 2018